Pastor Stevens has created a biblical paradigm for the African American church and the Jewish people to work together in supporting Israel. Using a scriptural foundation will have a more lasting affect in bringing the two faith communities closer than shared painful memories in its integration into American society.

—RABBI DR. SHLOMO RISKIN
Chief rabbi of Efrat, Israel
Founder, Center for Jewish-Christian
Understanding and Cooperation

Pastor Michael Stevens in this remarkable book has joined the chorus of courageous and passionate-for-truth Christian heroes standing in support of Israel. He is traveling the world to preach his courageous message. His voice resonates from America to Africa.

African Americans and Jewish communities working together could, through our shared past experiences with discrimination and oppression, bring the world closer to redemption. But this can happen only when the truth about the Jewish state of Israel prevails.

It is most appropriate then that at this time, when Israel is constantly under attack, being unjustly demonized, maligned, and delegitimized, that the African American community should stand together in support of Israel.

I thank Pastor Stevens for writing this much-needed book, for not standing idly by when his brothers and sisters are threatened.

—RABBI ARYEH SCHEINBERG
Leader of Congregation Rodfei Sholom
in San Antonio, Texas
Rabbinic adviser for Christians United for Israel

WE TOO
STAND

MICHAEL A. STEVENS, DMin

Cover design by Justin Evans
Design Director: Bill Johnson

Visit the author's website at www.UniversityCityChurch.tv.

Library of Congress Cataloging-in-Publication Data:
Stevens, Michael A.
 We too stand / Michael Stevens.
     pages ; cm
 Includes bibliographical references and index.
  ISBN 978-1-62136-231-9 (trade paper) -- ISBN 978-1-62136-
232-6 (ebook)
 1. African American churches. 2. African Americans--
Religion. 3. African Americans--Relations with Jews. 4.
African Americans--Attitudes. 5. Public opinion--Israel. 6.
Christian Zionism. 7. United States--Race relations. I. Title.
  BR563.N4S746 2013
  261.2'6--dc23
                                        2013001034

While the author has made every effort to provide accurate
telephone numbers and Internet addresses at the time of
publication, neither the publisher nor the author assumes
any responsibility for errors or for changes that occur after
publication.

First edition

13 14 15 16 17 — 987654321
Printed in the United States of America

A WORD TO ARAB PALESTINIAN CHRISTIANS

"For I know the plans I have for you," declares the LORD, "plans to prosper you and not to harm you, plans to give you hope and a future."
—JEREMIAH 29:11

To BE PRO-ISRAEL does not equate with being anti-Palestinian. To stand with Israel does not mean to stand against the many forgotten Arab Christians in the Middle East. There are approximately eight million people in Israel, the Holy Land of the Bible. Unfortunately, living there are the forgotten people in the Middle East. I think of them as a minority among minorities—they are our brothers and sisters in the Christian faith: Palestinian Christians.

These Arab believers are stuck in a no-win situation. For a people who make up less than 1.5 percent of the population in the Middle East, Palestinian Christians are faced with continuing pain, pressure, and persecution. In a city like Jerusalem they find themselves alienated on all sides. Most Jews shun them, angered by the Christians' message that Jesus is the Messiah who has already come, died for their sins, and rose again. Muslims too dislike being told that Jesus is the Christ and the only way to heaven. Catholics aren't fond of these Christians either because they stand as an ever-present reminder that the just shall live by faith through grace, not works. Finally, we Christian Zionists sometimes demonstrate insensitivity and inattentiveness toward them in our zeal to advance biblical and theological objectives in support of Israel.

Recently I had the privilege of meeting Pastor Steven Khoury, a Palestinian Christian and community leader. The director of Holy Land Missions (www.holylandmissions.org), he also leads several significant churches in Israel. Like many Christian Zionists I am also committed to praying and serving as a strong voice for Pastor Khoury, his churches, and other faithful Arab Christians living in the birthplace of our Messiah, Jesus Christ. I encourage him and all of our other persecuted Christian brothers around the world with the words of the apostle Paul: having done all—stand! (Eph. 6:13).

—DR. MICHAEL A. STEVENS SR.

CONTENTS

FOREWORD

JESUS OF NAZARETH said of John the Baptist—a forerunner of divine revelation: "What did you go out into the wilderness to see? A reed shaken by the wind?" (Luke 7:24, NKJV).

John the Baptist was a voice—not an echo!

In his moving, comprehensive, and engaging book, Dr. Michael Stevens offers a voice and not an echo to his generation. He does this in the same way that John the Baptist confronted his generation with truth. Like John the Baptist Dr. Stevens represents a forerunner to the African American community. In the spirit of revelation he explains why and how Christians should support Israel and why Israel has the right to exist and the right to defend itself.

Dietrich Bonhoeffer, the courageous pastor, martyr, prophet, and spy who resisted Adolf Hitler and his Third Reich, once declared that silence in the face of evil is itself evil. This means that God will not hold those who remain silent without guilt. In other words, to not speak is to speak, and avoiding action is to act.

In this book, Dr. Stevens breaks an oft-prevalent silence concerning Israel. In doing so, he challenges Christians everywhere to receive this biblical revelation of truth.

—PASTOR JOHN HAGEE

John C. Hagee is senior pastor of Cornerstone Church in San Antonio, Texas; founder of Christians United for Israel (CUFI); and author of several books, including Jerusalem Countdown *and* In Defense of Israel.

FOREWORD

D R. MICHAEL A. Stevens simply gets it! He has passionately hit the nail on the head with this book. It belongs in every pastor's library and should be part of every ministry and leadership instructor's resource arsenal. If there has ever been a time for the African American church to stand with and support Israel and the Jewish community, now is the time! Today Israel is facing its most critical moments since it became a state. Hamas, Hezbollah, and the tyrannical leadership of Iran have all expressed their desire to rid the world of a Jewish presence. In America many suggest that anti-Semitism is quickly growing among African Americans—something the Jewish community finds interesting since many Jews stood with African Americans during the civil rights era of the 1960s.

The African American church can and must make a difference. This book promises to accurately inform and instruct the Christian community on the increasing importance of supporting Israel with prayers and a unified presence. Dr. Stevens also gives several practical motives and reasons the Christians church—namely the African American church—may lay aside its differences with the Jewish community and embrace its biblical mandate to support the Jewish people.

—BISHOP HARRY R. JACKSON

Bishop Harry R. Jackson is senior pastor of Hope Christian Church in Beltsville, Maryland, and chairman of the High Impact Leadership Coalition. He recently formed the International Communion of Evangelical Churches, a network of more than 1,200 churches around the world. He is the author of several books, including Personal Faith, Public Policy *(which he coauthored with Tony Perkins) and* The Truth in Black and White.

PREFACE

ONE OF THE world's greatest tragedies took place in Europe during the 1930s and 1940s. Some six million Jews were imprisoned, tortured, and systematically murdered in a campaign that has become known as the Holocaust. I wish I could look back at that time in history and point to a glimmer of hope arising from the Christian church in the United States. But, sadly, many in the American church remained sheepishly silent while Adolf Hitler led the German campaign of Nazism and anti-Semitism throughout Europe.

According to a survey conducted in the late 1930s, more than 95 percent of Germans alive then considered themselves Christians and belonged to a Christian church.[1] It was with the support of the Catholic Church and other Christian groups in Germany that Hitler and his followers moved to annihilate the Jewish people.

Like the German church, American Christians share responsibility for the Holocaust through their involvement with an anti-Semitic view known as "replacement theology." Proponents of this theology teach that the church has essentially replaced Israel in God's plan and that the many promises made to Israel in Scripture are fulfilled in the Christian church. They claim that instead of being His chosen people, the Jewish nation has no specific role in God's future plans.

Many church leaders today recognize that this theology did more to help than hinder the gross injustice perpetuated during the Holocaust. In his book *Standing With Israel*, author David Brog notes: "Much like the Catholic Church, the Protestant world has through its actions recognized the connection between replacement theology and the horror of the Holocaust. In the aftermath of the Holocaust, most major Protestant denominations have adopted resolutions clearly renouncing this teaching."[2]

Brog writes that the Evangelical Lutheran Church in Germany took the lead in changing its theological course, declaring in 1950, "God's promise is valid for his Chosen People, even after the crucifixion of Jesus Christ."[3] The American Lutheran Church soon followed suit, as did most of the major Protestant denominations in America.[4]

Elliott Abrams, the author of *Faith or Fear*, notes that when the Presbyterian Church rejected replacement theology in 1987, it acknowledged that it was "agonizing to discover that the church's teaching of contempt [for the Jews] was a major ingredient that made possible the monstrous policy of annihilation of Jews by Nazi Germany."[5]

Although the link between replacement theology and the horror of the Holocaust has been acknowledged, this viewpoint, also called "fulfillment theology," is finding new life as memories of the Holocaust fade and pressure from Arab groups rises. Daniel Juster, director of Tikkun International and a founder of Messianic Jewish Bible Institute, writes, "After the Holocaust most major mainline denominations officially repudiated replacement theology, the largest being the Roman Catholic Church. But as the impact of the Holocaust has waned and these denominations have been influenced by Arab propaganda concerning Israel's treatment of the Palestinians, replacement attitudes and views have begun to resurface."[6]

As Israel faces threats to its existence from its bordering neighbors, the church cannot fall silent again. I believe if any Christians in America should stand with the Jewish people, it should be the African American church, given our communities' similar experiences of bondage, pain, and hardship. Almost 12 million Africans were taken captive and tortured during the slave trade between that continent and the Americas from the 1500s and 1800s.[7] Like the Jews taken captive during the Holocaust, millions of those Africans lost their lives.

Yet despite the parallels in our experiences, many African American churches feel no responsibility to support or stand with Israel. I believe this is partly due to misunderstandings about the history of the Israeli-Palestinian conflict, a lack of awareness of African American–Jewish relations during the civil rights movement, and, most importantly, an incomplete knowledge of what the Bible teaches about Israel.

As replacement theology quietly reenters the mainstream, many African American churches are feeling emboldened to ignore desperate solicitations of support for Israel and the Jewish community. But no matter what the popular rhetoric, the church has a biblical and theological responsibility to pray for and stand with Israel. As

Psalm 122:6 says, "Pray for the peace of Jerusalem! May they prosper who love you!" (RSV). Still today, the prophet Isaiah exhorts us with these words: "For Zion's sake I will not keep silent, and for Jerusalem's sake I will not rest, until her vindication goes forth as brightness, and her salvation as a burning torch....Upon your walls, O Jerusalem, I have set watchmen; all the day and all the night they shall never be silent. You who put the LORD in remembrance, take no rest, and give him no rest until he establishes Jerusalem and makes it a praise in the earth" (Isa. 62:1, 6–7, RSV).

I believe there is no other entity on earth that can most identify itself as a people with the Jews than the African American church. The African American church carries both a prophetic zeal and a historic resolve to boldly stand against the injustices and unrighteousness in the world. We are reminded in Scripture that "ambassadors will come from Egypt; Cush will stretch out its hands to God" (Ps. 68:31, HCSB). There is a mantle and mandate upon the African American church to demonstrate righteous leadership and influence beyond the confines of Sunday morning services and midweek Bible studies. The commonalities between two destined peoples—the African American and Jewish communities—are too obvious to overlook.

Not only is there an anti-Zionism campaign afoot, but there is also an anti-Israel campaign. In a speech delivered in Cairo, Egypt, in June of 2009, President Barack Obama reached out to the Muslim world and challenged all to repudiate the Holocaust denial stemming back to the days of Hitler. Today Israel needs the president of the United States to also courageously speak from Jerusalem and challenge Palestinians, Arabs, and Muslims to accept Israel's historic roots as a people and acknowledge its right to live in peace in its ancient homeland—the land of the Bible.

It is our responsibility as believers in Jesus to challenge our US government leaders to support the Jewish state. I pray that it will never again be said that the Jewish people suffered violently at the hands of an oppressor while the church remained silent. Instead of following the lead of mainline churches who disregard the unique part Israel plays in the plan and purposes of God, instead of joining the ranks of those who condemn or even vilify the efforts of Christian Zionists, I pray that from within the walls of African American churches across this nation the world will hear a voice rise up to declare, "We too stand!"

INTRODUCTION

O N OCTOBER 6, 1943, approximately four hundred Jewish rabbis courageously stood on the steps of the US Capitol, eagerly awaiting an audience with President Franklin D. Roosevelt (FDR). Their goal that morning was to seek assistance from the American government for millions of European Jews who were experiencing horrible persecution by the Nazis. Yet while the rabbis quietly marched in front of the White House, President Roosevelt slipped quietly out the back door.

According to the American Jewish Historical Society, "On the advice of his aides, FDR, who was scheduled to attend a military ceremony, intentionally avoided the rabbis by leaving the White House through a rear exit.... When Roosevelt's decision not to encounter the rabbis became known to the press, reporters interpreted Roosevelt's actions as a snub, adding a dramatic flair that transformed the protest rally into a full-fledged clash between the rabbis and the administration."[1]

When I read about this moment in history—when America missed an opportunity to do something truly heroic—I couldn't help but wonder, "Where were the Christians?" During Israel and the Jewish people's most pressing hour, where were the concerned clergy and ministry leaders?

I asked this in part because I knew another bit of history. In the 1960s African Americans were facing our greatest challenge since slavery was abolished. Beginning in the 1950s, we had effectively used public marches and demonstrations to change government policies that allowed African Americans to be treated unequally. There had been many marches throughout the South since then, but one in Selma, Alabama, in 1965 would stand out from the rest. In March of that year civil rights activists attempted to march from Selma to Montgomery to protest unfair voting practices. But as they reached the outskirts of Selma, state and local lawmen used clubs and tear gas to push them back to Selma.

Later that month Dr. Martin Luther King Jr. boldly led tens of thousands of demonstrators to finish what the other marchers had started.[2] As Dr. King and other civil rights leaders marched despite the threat of violence, an unlikely supporter fearlessly stood shoulder to shoulder with them. His name was Rabbi Abraham Joshua Heschel (1907–1972).[3] This Jewish leader felt he had an obligation to help those who were suffering, and it was this conviction that led him to courageously oppose the unequal treatment of African Americans.

In subsequent interviews Rabbi Heschel said the burden to get involved at the risk of his own safety was born of his reading of the Scriptures. "The more deeply immersed I became in the thinking of the prophets," he said, "the more powerfully it became clear to me what the lives of the prophets sought to convey: that morally speaking there is no limit to the concern one must feel for the suffering of human beings."[4] When he marched from Selma to Montgomery, Heschel said his "legs were praying."[5]

Rabbi Heschel was not the only Jew possessing such a sense of social responsibility. Historians estimate that one-third to one-half of the non-African Americans who participated in the historic Freedom Rides across the South in the 1960s were Jewish.[6]

Many Jewish attorneys sacrificed income to defend unjustly accused African Americans facing legal charges for standing for justice and civil rights. Jews also contributed financially to many of the key organizations standing for equality and fairness, another demonstration of its support for the African American community during the civil rights era.

This Jewish support for African American equality did not originate in the sixties. In 1909 a group of prominent individuals—including W. E. B. Du Bois, other noted African Americans, and several Jewish leaders—met in the home of Joel Spingarn, a Jewish man, to form the National Association for the Advancement of Colored People (NAACP).[7] Ironically, not until 1975 did the NAACP have its first African American president.[8]

In the early sixties civil rights organizations such as Student Nonviolent Coordinating Committee (SNCC) and the Congress for Racial Equality (CORE) were comprised of Jewish leaders as well as African Americans. More than 75 percent of the contributions flowing to SNCC and CORE came from Jews. These men and women helped organize the aptly named Freedom Rides, riding together on buses throughout the South with African Americans as they challenged numerous laws and practices that supported segregation and discrimination.[9]

We can all learn today from the example set by these concerned Jewish citizens. We should exhibit similar understanding of charity and obligation to help others in crisis. *Tzedakah* is the Hebrew word for charity. Early in life the Jewish people learn that they have a moral obligation to be charitable and help those dealing with social battles of justice and equality. Because of their unique history of facing struggle and injustice, the Jewish people fully comprehend why they had an obligation to boldly support their African American friends. The late Dr. Martin Luther King Jr. once said, "It would be impossible to record the contribution that Jewish people have made toward the Negro's struggle for freedom, it has been so great."[10]

There are unique similarities between the Jewish and African American communities. Both have suffered horrendous persecution and oppression as a people. From the millions of lives lost via the Africa-America slave trade to the six million Jews killed during the Holocaust, both groups can identify with the pain of being a people dislocated, disenfranchised, and disregarded.

Both groups also looked to a similar place to find meaning in the midst of their struggle. The biblical account of the Jewish exodus took on striking significance to African Americans during slavery as our prayers, sermons, and spiritual songs centered on the hope of deliverance to "Canaan Land"—a place of freedom. Harold

Brackman observes: "Though most Americans like to imagine our country [the United States] as 'a promised land,' the Hebrew Bible's narratives of redemption from slavery and oppression have provided a special spiritual roadmap for two communities: African Americans and Jews who have struggled—often as allies—for civil rights and inclusion in the American Dream."[11]

Israel's current, tenuous situation in the Middle East creates a new and unprecedented opportunity for African Americans and Jews to stand together. Israel's neighbor Iran is a determined and existential threat. At 650 times Israel's size, Iran is experiencing a "spring uprising," creating a hostile and uncomfortable dilemma for Israel. Both militant Palestinian groups Hamas and Hezbollah have plainly stated their objective is to annihilate Israel and the Jewish people. Pressures exist in the United States too. The White House and State Department want Israel to cede land and foreign policy.

It is 1943 all over again, and Israel needs help. This time the rabbis will not stand on the steps of the Capitol alone. Christian Zionism has awakened. I believe that in this determined group of believers will be many concerned, faithful, praying African Americans. Why? Because we appreciate history, because we consider the Jewish people our friends, and because we too understand *tzedakah*.

Chapter 1

WHY SUPPORT ISRAEL?

I N THE SUMMER of 2000 my wife and I visited the Holy Land with a small group of graduate students and college professors. Like most Christians, and especially as a pastor, I had always wanted to see Israel. However, at the time I didn't realize the personal significance this nation would assume in my life. Seven years later, during a time of prayer and Bible study, the Lord placed on my heart the blessings that stem from supporting Israel and standing with it.

As I studied Genesis 12, God opened my eyes and gave emphatic instructions for my young black Pentecostal church and myself. I sensed Him saying we were to bless Israel and the Jewish people, and I was directed to this passage:

> The LORD had said to Abram, "Leave your country, your people and your father's household and go to the land I will show you. I will make you into a great nation and I will bless you; I will make your name great, and you will be a blessing. I will bless those who bless you, and whoever curses you I

> will curse; and all peoples on earth will be blessed
> through you."
>
> —GENESIS 12:1–3

That same weekend, during three morning worship services, I shared with the congregation what I believed the Lord had prophetically revealed to me. As the Old Testament states, "Surely the Lord GOD will do nothing, but he revealeth his secret unto his servants the prophets" (Amos 3:7, KJV). I told the congregation I believed God had instructed me to befriend the Jewish people and stand with them, offering prayer and moral support. There was just one problem: I had no Jewish friends and had never been inside a Jewish synagogue or associated with Jews, with the exception of shopping on Lower Manhattan's East Side, an area populated by discount stores and Orthodox-owned men's clothing shops.

Despite my lack of familiarity with the Jewish community, within thirty days of my pronouncement I spoke at the annual convention of my denomination, the Church of God in Christ. There I met nationally known pastor John Hagee and his wife, Diana, who were speaking to the delegates before hosting a book signing. At the time, the mutual friend who introduced me to the Hagees was also soliciting help for a startup organization called Christians United for Israel (CUFI).

The organization just happened to need assistance in North Carolina, where I lived. I recognized this was no coincidence. I had heard from the Lord, with this vision sealed and affirmed by friends and members of my church, and now the Lord was opening an effective door for ministry.

Six months later, during a church leaders' "familiarization tour" of Israel, Pastor Hagee and I talked about the scores of African American Christians who believed in supporting Israel. Many of these believers remember hearing while growing up in church that they should bless and love Israel and the Jewish people. Many heard their pastors instruct them to keep their eyes on the "fig tree," which speaks prophetically of the importance of Israel in the end times (Matt. 24:32). As we talked, I expressed the need to build on this good foundation to motivate and mobilize African American Christians nationwide in a unified commitment to support Israel. Pastor Hagee agreed; this vision has been coming to pass ever since.

Biblical Reasons to Support Israel

There are many reasons Christians should support Israel. The two most important are: (1) the biblical, and (2) the moral.

First, a thorough, comprehensive grasp of what the Bible says about Israel will lead a person to support the Jewish nation. As Bible-believing Christians we have a divine mandate to encourage and support Israel. The Old Testament expresses the unique commitment the Lord has to the children of Israel, His beloved people. His overarching plan and promise include not just blessing Israel but also those who support it.

As I mentioned at the beginning of this chapter, the passage from Genesis 12 that made such an impression on me ends with God telling Abram, "I will bless those who bless you, and whoever curses you I will curse; and all peoples on earth will be blessed through you" (Gen. 12:3). You may ask: Why Abram? Why Israel? What great purpose was God calling Abram to?

The first Hebrew patriarch, whose name means "Father is exalted," would become known as the prime example of faith.[1] While he was living in Haran, Abram at the age of seventy-five received a call from God to go to a unknown land that God would show him. The Lord promised to make Abram and his descendants into a great nation, which seemed unbelievable to Abram and his wife because they were childless and advanced in years. Yet Abram obeyed God, and in time God fulfilled His promise.

Scripture tells us in Romans 4:18–21:

> Against all hope, Abraham in hope believed and so became the father of many nations, just as it had been said to him, "So shall your offspring be." Without weakening in his faith, he faced the fact that his body was as good as dead—since he was about a hundred years old—and that Sarah's womb was also dead. Yet he did not waver through unbelief regarding the promise of God, but was strengthened in his faith and gave glory to God, being fully persuaded that God had power to do what he had promised.

The purpose of God (or Yahweh, as the Jews know Him) in calling Abram was to benefit more than just one person or one family. God's invitation to Abram represents His invitation to a people who would exist not just for a generation but for all eternity. As E. A. Speiser writes, "The story commences with one individual, and extends gradually to his family, then to a people, and later still to a nation... it is to be the story of a society in quest of an ideal."[2] God called Abram, whom He later renamed Abraham, to a promised land that would eventually be a part of God's covenantal agreement with His people, Israel.

In Genesis 13:17 God says to Abram, "Go, walk through the length and breadth of the land, for I am giving it to you." At that time Canaan was inhabited by a warlike people, so Abram's belief that God would give this land to him and his descendants was indeed an act of faith. Though the circumstances seemed difficult, Abram had confidence in God's promises. He agreed to go to the land that God would show him, and God agreed to honor his obedience by making Abram a great nation. This act is partly what made Abram a "man of the covenant and spiritual father of both Jews and Christians," as Bible scholar and seminary professor Marvin R. Wilson writes.[3] In time God's promise of salvation would come to Israel in the person of Jesus Christ, with an invitation to partake in that salvation extended to the Gentiles.

The fact that God had especially chosen the people of Israel became central to their identity, writes British New Testament scholar James D. G. Dunn. "Equally fundamental to Israel's self-understanding was its conviction that it had been specially chosen by Yahweh," he says, "that the one God had bound himself to Israel and Israel to

himself by a special contract, or *covenant*."⁴ This is clearly
evident in the message Moses chronicled in Deuteronomy:

> For you are a people holy to the LORD your God.
> The LORD your God has chosen you out of all the
> peoples on the face of the earth to be his people,
> his treasured possession. The LORD did not set his
> affection on you and choose you because you were
> more numerous than other peoples, for you were
> the fewest of all peoples. But it was because the
> LORD loved you and kept the oath he swore to your
> forefathers that he brought you out with a mighty
> hand and redeemed you from the land of slavery,
> from the power of Pharaoh king of Egypt. Know
> therefore that the LORD your God is God; he is
> the faithful God, keeping his covenant of love to
> a thousand generations of those who love him and
> keep his commands.
>
> —DEUTERONOMY 7:6–9

God established His commitment to Israel through a
series of promises to Abram, saying He would curse those
who cursed His children or showed contempt for them.
Genesis 12:1–3 reveals three important truths:

1. The promise that God makes with Abram
   and the children of Israel is eternal and
   everlasting.

2. The children of Israel are God's special
   people (Gen. 15:1–7).

3. The promise of blessings the Lord would grant to Abram and his supporters is as active today as it was thousands of years ago.

As Wilson notes, "The Hebrews were God's 'treasured possession,' a living 'kingdom of priests' (Ex. 19:5–6)."[5] For Moses the promises God made to Israel were more than just gestures or wishful intentions; minister and seminary professor W. Eugene March says God's commitment to the Jews was "an agreement or contract akin to a marriage, a compact, an adoption decree, or a political treaty."[6] It is also important to note that God makes a *promise* to Abram in Genesis 12. The children of Israel would be *in covenant* with God, but the passage in Genesis 12 speaks of the *promise* God makes to them.

The word *covenant* means "a pact, treaty, alliance, or agreement between two parties of equal or of unequal authority."[7] Concerning God's covenant and the children of Israel, Wilson writes, "Within the Biblical concept of covenant, Judaism sees at least four pillars upon which it rests: God, Torah, the people of Israel, and the land of Israel, each one depending on and interacting with the others."[8] God's covenant of promises to Abram was not due to his perfection or good works, but because of God's grace and intended purposes for Abram's life.

The *Holman Bible Dictionary* observes, "The covenant with Abraham, like with Noah, involved divine promises, not human obedience."[9] The covenant God made with Abram and the Israelites in those days is the same continuing, everlasting binding agreement God makes with those who willfully obey His Word today. This covenant is as much in existence now as it was in the days of Abram.

God's Indelible Imprint

The biblical narrative about Abram conveys the importance of God's covenant of promises to both the father of Israel and those who would bless His nation and Abram's descendants. When Moses writes about Israel in Genesis 12, he wants readers to realize that this is more than a geographical nation or ethnic tribe with religious ties. This was a nation of people who bore God's everlasting, unchanging commitment—a kind of indelible imprint.

In Genesis 12 Moses employs the term *barak*, meaning "to bless," "to kneel," or "to bow." According to the *Anchor Bible Dictionary*, *barak* "can have a diverse but unrelated etymological meaning.…Bless/blessing has been most frequently understood in terms of benefits conveyed— prosperity, power, and especially fertility."[10] The original Hebraic term Moses uses means that God would endue with power for success, prosperity, fecundity, and longevity.[11] God's blessings are often manifested in prosperity and well-being. Long life, wealth, peace, good harvest, and children appear frequently on lists of blessings. (See Leviticus 26:4–13; Deuteronomy 28:3–15.) This is true today; if we bless Israel, God will bless and prosper us in return.

Examples of individuals in the Old Testament who were blessed with protection and prosperity for blessing Abraham's descendants included Laban, the father-in-law of Abraham's grandson Jacob, whose name was changed to Israel: "But Laban said to him, 'If I have found favor in your eyes, please stay. I have learned by divination that the LORD has blessed me because of you'" (Gen. 30:27).

Later we see the extension of this blessing to Jacob's son Joseph: "From the time he put him in charge of his household and of all that he owned, the LORD blessed the household of the Egyptian because of Joseph. The blessing of the LORD was on everything Potiphar had, both in the house and in the field" (Gen. 39:5). Recognizing the intention of God's covenant and blessing on Israel should compel us to show support for this nation.

One way twenty-first-century believers can bless Israel is by praying for this nation and its people. Throughout the Bible prayer is a central theme and common practice. In the preface I mentioned the directive in Psalm 122:6 that we are to pray for the peace of Jerusalem. In Isaiah 62:1–7 God calls the prophet to act as a watchman for Israel, to ensure its protection and prosperity:

> For Zion's sake I will not keep silent,
>> for Jerusalem's sake I will not remain quiet,
> till her righteousness shines out like the dawn,
>> her salvation like a blazing torch.
> The nations will see your righteousness,
>> and all kings your glory;
> you will be called by a new name
>> that the mouth of the LORD will bestow.
> You will be a crown of splendor in the LORD's
>> hand,
>> a royal diadem in the hand of your God.
> No longer will they call you Deserted,
>> or name your land Desolate.

But you will be called Hephzibah,
    and your land Beulah;
for the LORD will take delight in you,
    and your land will be married.
As a young man marries a maiden,
    so will your sons marry you;
as a bridegroom rejoices over his bride,
    so will your God rejoice over you.
I have posted watchmen on your walls, O
     Jerusalem;
    they will never be silent day or night.
You who call on the LORD,
    give yourselves no rest,
and give him no rest till he establishes Jerusalem
    and makes her the praise of the earth.

The prophet Isaiah represents all the people of God who love and will intercede for "Zion." Why would God need Isaiah, or us for that matter, to "never be silent day or night" and "giving him no rest" until He fulfills His promise to Israel? Seminary professor John Oswalt writes: "One might ask why God would need to be reminded of his promises, but that is to read the imagery in an overly literal way. God is asserting that he will never forget what he has promised, no matter how dark the days may become between the hour the prophet speaks it and the day of its fulfillment."[12] Israel needs our prayers, but that is not because it is no longer under God's care. No matter how much time spans between His promise and its fulfillment, God will never forget His people. As Oswalt notes, just to be sure He does not forget, God appoints people as "reminders" who will say, "Lord, don't forget what You said about Jerusalem." He will not give Himself rest, and will not allow those who remind Him to give Him rest, until His plans for Jerusalem are accomplished.

Christians today are called to support Israel, both by serving as watchmen on the wall and speaking out about its welfare, remembering that Israel remains under God's care. As nineteenth-century theologians Carl Keil and Franz Delitzsch wrote, "Jehovah gives to the restored Jerusalem faithful prophets, whom He stations upon the walls of the city, that they may see far and wide, and be heard afar off. And from those walls does their warning cry on behalf of the holy city committed to their care ascend day and night to Jehovah, and their testimony go round about to the world."[13]

Ever since the days of the legendary prophet God has appointed faithful pastors, ministers, and Christian leaders to tend to the walls of spiritual Zion. Warning the citizens of sin and error, they are in constant prayer for the land and its people. These watchmen are helping fulfill the Lord's pledge in Isaiah 62:8–9 that never again would Zion's food and drink fall into the hands of its enemies:

> The LORD has sworn by his right hand
>   and by his mighty arm:
> "Never again will I give your grain
>   as food for your enemies,
> and never again will foreigners drink the new wine
>   for which you have toiled;
> but those who harvest it will eat it
>   and praise the LORD,

and those who gather the grapes will drink it
in the courts of my sanctuary."

According to Isaiah, the children of Israel (or Zion) were to be the initial, direct recipients of God's covenant promise, but they were not the only ones. For Isaiah, Zion is not only the capital of Judah but also the dwelling place of God. So too the Gentiles who turn to Him participate in this covenant promise. These same Gentiles and their leaders would take note of Zion's change of fortune and blessings (vv. 2–3); they would see the handiwork of God— His goodness toward His prized possession. The Lord would commemorate the new circumstances by bestowing a special name on His people: "No longer will they call you Deserted, or name your land Desolate. But you will be called Hephzibah, and your land Beulah; for the LORD will take delight in you" (v. 4).

The renovated and renewed people of God would be glorious, like a crown embellished and admired by a king. For Zion had previously been forsaken and desolate; however, the Lord gave His people new names, showing the same unconditional love for Zion that a bridegroom exhibits for his bride. Say professors Bill Arnold and Bryan Beyer: "Today, a bride generally assumes her husband's name. The name change signifies the beginning of a new special relationship. God also had new names chosen for His bride (Is. 62:4). Hephzibah means 'my delight is in her' and Beulah means, 'married.' The Lord rejoices in his people as a bridegroom rejoiced in his bride. What a picture of God's love."[14]

Isaiah again refers to the people of God as Zion in the concluding chapter of his book: "Who has ever heard of such a thing? Who has ever seen such things? Can a country be born in a day or a nation be brought forth in a moment? Yet no sooner is Zion in labor than she gives birth to her children" (Isa. 66:8).

In a parallel way the Book of Revelation also compares God's covenant with Zion to a bride and marriage: "Then I saw a new heaven and a new earth, for the first heaven and the first earth had passed away, and there was no longer any sea. I saw the Holy City, the new Jerusalem, coming down out of heaven from God, prepared as a bride beautifully dressed for her husband" (Rev. 21:1–2). First Peter indicates God's intention for Zion as well: "But you are a chosen people, a royal priesthood, a holy nation, a people belonging to God, that you may declare the praises of him who called you out of darkness into his wonderful light" (1 Pet. 2:9).

Fitting With God's Plan

As we interpret Isaiah's prophecy concerning Israel's watchmen, theological research becomes crucial in understanding the main themes and purposes of Isaiah 62:1–7. Where does this passage of Scripture fit in the overarching plan of God and revelation as it relates to believers today supporting Israel? It is clear in this passage that the prophet communicated both his desire and Yahweh's intention to extend His redemption and salvation to Israel, His covenant people. This covenant has been secured with the placement of watchmen on the walls, individuals who are committed to standing with Zion and speaking forth for the sake of its security. This aligns with God's comprehensive plan for Israel recorded throughout Scripture. (See Deuteronomy 26:18–19; Ezekiel 3:17; Hosea 2:19–20.) Here are some key points about how the Isaiah passage relates to our situation today:

The prophet spoke these words in a specific historical situation.

However, there are valid interpretations for today's culture and environment.

As previously mentioned, there is a dual objective with the prophetic declaration. The message for the people of Israel is the same message for the church today. As Old Testament professor Douglas Stuart observes: "Does the passage have a double–barreled application, as certain messianic passages do—one application having immediate reference for the people who first heard it in OT times, the other having more of a long-range reference, for people in our day?"[15] Clearly it does.

It is my personal and theological opinion that Isaiah saw something prophetic concerning Israel's current situation as well as its future state. Because God's promises and covenants were eternal and everlasting, salvation and refuge would come to the Jewish people despite their backsliding and wayward ways. They would not always be labeled or identified as deserted or desolate; God would again make them the royal diadem in His hand. Peeking into the future prophetically, God has an overarching plan of salvation for the Jewish people, and that salvation is found in the Messiah, Jesus the Christ.

I believe that in the end times God will usher in an incredible invitation to the Jewish nation to acknowledge the salvation that came through Christ's cross. To ensure and safeguard this thought, I believe today it is the modern-day watchmen on the wall who, perhaps, Israel foresaw who are to demonstrate true love, sincere compassion, and authentic commitment to Israel's peace, safety, and security. It is my belief and conviction that for years Christians' hate drove the Jews away from Christ, but today the love of Christians is warmly drawing Jews back to their Messiah, Jesus the Christ.

This passage would be considered *principlist* in approach.

With this unique approach an attempt is made to identify transcultural principles that express for today's church the God-given principle behind the original command. The single, most direct message to Israel was that Yahweh has made an everlasting, unchanging covenant with them. To maintain it, He would ensure the presence of watchmen on the wall who would not remain silent or hold their peace. Yahweh also has an expectation that His covenant nation become a people of royalty and redemption—but that would come only if they accept His salvation.

Today's church can come to understand the passage's prophetic and messianic aspects.

While the prophet Isaiah prophetically spoke directly to Israel, his words contain a word of encouragement and strength for all who heed its redemptive and reassuring message. Look at one earlier prophecy:

> It shall come to pass in the latter days
>   that the mountain of the house of the LORD
> shall be established as the highest of the
>   mountains,
>   and shall be raised above the hills;
> and all the nations shall flow to it,
>   and many peoples shall come, and say:
> "Come, let us go up to the mountain of the LORD,
>   to the house of the God of Jacob;
> that he may teach us his ways
>   and that we may walk in his paths."
> For out of Zion shall go forth the law,
>   and the word of the LORD from Jerusalem.
>   —ISAIAH 2:2–3, RSV

Appreciating the full depth of Scripture in contemplating Israel yields a stunning picture of an eternal love affair between God and His people. As professors Arnold and Beyer write: "Isaiah foresaw a grand marriage between the Lord God and Zion, his bride. His prophecy provides a beautiful picture of God's love for his people and a foreshadowing of Christ's marriage to the church."[16] Today's church can possess confidence in knowing that Yahweh's unchanging love continues because He is the same yesterday, today, and forever (Heb. 13:8). He placed His love upon Zion, the firstborn and covenant people of God, in the days of the prophet Isaiah, and it is still there today.

Isaiah 62:1–7 serves as a strong argument for the church to stand with Israel. This passage and others offer biblical, theological, and moral motives. As the exclusive ministers of salvation, church leaders carry the awesome responsibility of courageously standing for the peace, security, and prosperity of God's covenant people. To summarize the major reasons for support found in this passage: there can be no silence (v. 1), no premature rest (v. 1), and no allowance to forsake or reject Israel (v. 4). As watchmen we must stand boldly and not hold our peace.

During His time on earth Jesus furthered this theme by referring to His disciples as "the light of the world" and "a city on a hill" (Matt. 5:14). This idea of supporting Israel appears in other New Testament passages, such as this one from Luke:

> Now a centurion had a slave who was dear to him, who was sick and at the point of death. When he heard of Jesus, he sent to him elders of the Jews, asking him to come and heal his slave. And when they came to Jesus, they besought him earnestly, saying, "He is worthy to have you do this for him, for he loves our nation, and he built us our synagogue."
>
> —Luke 7:2–5, rsv

It is obvious that this Roman centurion was a Gentile. Yet he loved Israel so dearly that he built their people a synagogue. Professor and author Craig Keener notes: "Non-Jews who feared God and donated substantial sums to the Jewish community were well respected. Centurions' salaries were much higher than those of their troops, but for this centurion to have built the local synagogue represented a great financial sacrifice."[17] Though this centurion considered himself unworthy of the Messiah's visit, his love and support of the Jewish nation attracted Christ's attention—and led to his servant's healing.

Christ's Brethren

In the same way Moses referenced a unique, covenant relationship between God and the children of Israel in Genesis 12, Matthew records Jesus using the phrase "My brethren" in the New Testament to describe a special covenant relationship:

> Then the righteous will answer Him, saying, "Lord, when did we see You hungry and feed You, or thirsty and give You drink? When did we see You a stranger and take You in, or naked and clothe You? Or when did we see You sick, or in prison, and come to You?" And the King will answer and say to them, "Assuredly, I say to you, inasmuch as you did it to one of the least of these My brethren, you did it to Me."
> —MATTHEW 25:37–40, NKJV

The Greek word for "brethren" denotes a physical brotherhood relationship. In a stricter sense it could also mean a spiritual brotherhood. Michael J. Wilkins—a professor of New Testament language and literature—points this out in commenting on Matthew 12:46–50, where Jesus remarks that whoever does His Father's will is related to the Christ. While His physical mother and brothers wait outside to see Him, Jesus stretches out His hand toward His disciples, or spiritual brothers, and says, "Here are my mother and my brothers. For whoever does the will of my Father in heaven is my brother and sister and mother" (vv. 49–50). Says Wilkins: "With this definition Jesus declares that spiritual union in the family of God takes precedence over national or blood-family lines (Luke 14:26)."[18]

This is important because of opposing perspectives about whether God's covenant with the children of Israel still existed in the New Testament. In Matthew 25 Jesus is asking the church to do something in support of His brethren, who are as much the people of Israel as they are the poor. When the church supports Israel, it is doing something for Him. Observes Keener: "In some Jewish apocalyptic texts, the nations would be judged for how they treated Israel. In the Bible, God also judged people for how they treated the poor."[19]

Some leading scholars and theologians believe that in using "My brethren" Christ intended to reinforce Israel as the beneficiary of an everlasting *relationship of continuity* with His Father. Such a view helped fuel mainstream Christians' favoritism toward Zionism and support for Israel—they recognized that the Jews were the biblical heirs and beneficiaries of Israel's land. March adds in his book *Great Themes of the Bible*, "New Testament writers continued to refer to Israelites and Jews as God's people, *laos*, distinguishing them from the nations, *ethnos*...there was no question whether the Judean community continued to be God's people."[20]

The apostle Paul affirms their status: "For I could wish that I myself were cursed and cut off from Christ for the sake of my brothers, those of my own race, the people of Israel. Theirs is the adoption as sons; theirs the divine glory, the covenants, the receiving of the law, the temple worship and the promises. Theirs are the patriarchs, and from them is traced the human ancestry of Christ, who is God over all, forever praised! Amen" (Rom. 9:3–5).

In the Gospels Jesus referenced Israel at the end of one of His parables: "From the fig tree learn its lesson: as soon as its branch becomes tender and puts forth its leaves, you know that summer is near. So also, when you see all these things, you know that he is near, at the very gates. Truly, I say to you, this generation will not pass away till all these things take place" (Matt. 24:32–34, rsv).

Jesus used this parable, which concerns Israel, to teach His disciples and the crowd that followed Him to maintain the correct perspective of God's everlasting covenant with the nation. Itinerant Bible teacher Lance Lambert, a British native living in Jerusalem, agrees: "I believe that the Lord Jesus was referring to this 'immortality' of the Jewish people when he said: 'From the fig tree learn its lesson.'…The lesson we are to learn is surely not merely about the coming of summer, but concerns that Jewish people, their land, statehood and destiny."[21]

In a different parable referring to a fig tree, Jesus's words can refer to the Messiah's coming for both Israel and the Gentile world:

> And he told this parable: "A man had a fig tree
> planted in his vineyard; and he came seeking
> fruit on it and found none. And he said to the
> vinedresser, 'Lo, these three years I have come
> seeking fruit on this fig tree, and I find none. Cut
> it down; why should it use up the ground?' And he
> answered him, 'Let it alone, sir, this year also, till
> I dig about it and put on manure. And if it bears
> fruit next year, well and good; but if not, you can
> cut it down.'"
>
> —LUKE 13:6–9, RSV

Says Joseph Fitzmyer of this passage: "It should be recalled that a fig tree often stood in the Old Testament as a symbol of Judah or Israel (Hos. 9:10; Mic. 7:1; Jer. 8:13; 24:1–10)."[22] In his comments on this passage, Lambert notes, "The Lord Jesus was clearly referring to himself and to the three years of the messianic ministry."[23] Israel is summoned to a covenantal relationship with the Messiah in both the New Testament and the Old Testament.

Indeed, when Christ commissioned His disciples in Matthew 10:5–6, He said He was sending them to evangelize "the lost sheep of Israel." Say authors W. F. Albright and C. S. Mann in their commentary on the Book of Matthew: "The commission here means that those so commissioned are to give absolute priority to those towns or areas where there are already Jewish settlements (cf. vs. 23), as areas where the Messianic message would not be foreign."[24] Fitzmyer writes, "All, both Jews with their covenantal uprightness and Gentiles with their lack of uprightness, are accosted by the gospel of God's uprightness; they can all react to it in faith."[25] He continues, "The priority of the Jew is acknowledged not only because the gospel was first preached to the Jews, but because God promised his gospel through the prophets of old in the sacred Scriptures of the Jews."[26]

The Moral Imperative

As I mentioned earlier in this chapter, the second dominant reason that Christians should stand with Israel stems from a moral, ethical perspective. While in recent times anti-Semitic voices have obscured the truth, this obligation originated in the first-century church, when Paul expressed his support for the Jewish people: "They were pleased to do it, and indeed they are in debt to them, for if the Gentiles have come to share in their spiritual blessings, they ought also to be of service to them in material blessings" (Rom. 15:27, RSV). Those are significant words; we who follow Christ are indebted to the Jewish people! The Christian church has received from them the *Tanakh*, the Jewish Bible (Old Testament), as well the patriarchs Abraham, Isaac, and Jacob and prophets such as Daniel, Elijah, and Isaiah.

Most significantly Christians received from a little town in Bethlehem the Jewish Messiah—Jesus, the Christ. Christianity's roots and origins lie in a Jewish foundation. Without Judaism and the Scriptures, there would be no Christianity. Therefore Christians today have a responsibility to support Israel, particularly in a time of its greatest need. Walid Shoebat, a former radical Muslim turned Christian, writes, "This command (Romans 15:27) reveals the increasing opportunities to reach out to the Jewish people and speak a prophetic word concerning God's desire for them."[27]

Scholars Robert Haldane, James Dunn, and N. T. Wright all have commented on how Romans 15:27 emphasizes the gift of unity. Perhaps more than financial or material gain for the Jewish leaders in Jerusalem, it seems Paul's explicit desire for those in Rome was that they experience the blessing of communion and unity. Says Haldane: "They [the Gentiles] were debtors to the Jews for the Gospel. Not only did the kingdom of God first originate with the Jews, but it was through the instrumentality of Jews that the Gentiles received it. They carried it to their doors, and besought them to receive the blessing. From this we may learn the extent of the obligation, and the unity of the body of Christ."[28]

For Dunn the apostle Paul clearly gives the rationale for the collection commonly taken for the leadership in Jerusalem. (See 2 Corinthians 1–7.) Dunn says that "Gentiles have come to share in Israel's spiritual blessings; for such Gentiles to share their material blessings with the saints in Jerusalem was a quite proper act of gratitude and brotherly concern...no doubt also he would hope thereby to consolidate the Gentile mission in the eyes of the Jerusalem leadership."[29]

Wright sees this "united family" as Paul's worldview concerning Judaism and the Christian faith: "But I have come to the conclusion that the central symbol of Paul's worldview is the united community: Jew-Greek, slave-free, male-female: the one family of Abraham, the family for the world, the single family created anew in Jesus Christ from people of every kind."[30]

Besides the moral imperative, standing with Israel in prayer and solidarity is politically strategic. I have no doubt that a primary reason the United States has enjoyed prosperity and the blessing of freedom is the Judeo-Christian values and principles that undergird our nation. Many Christians agree with me that another reason is our continued partnership with Israel, the greatest democracy in the Middle East. God's sovereign hand of grace and protection doesn't stem from our purity or worthiness, but from adhering to His promise to Abraham in Genesis 12:1–3. We must recognize that supporting Israel invokes the blessings of Abraham, Isaac, and Jacob upon our lives—for it is in Israel that these blessings rest.

Chapter 2

UNDERSTANDING CHRISTIAN ZIONISM

A FRICAN AMERICAN CHURCHES and Jewish people share similar convictions and core beliefs regarding the significance of the Jews' return to their historic homeland. Despite this, *Zionism* and *Christian Zionism* are generally unfamiliar terms in African American church circles. Because those terms are seldom referenced in our settings and are not part of typical conversations, many within our community view this movement as having a political agenda. They see it as comprised primarily of white "Rapture-ready," pretribulation evangelicals eagerly desiring Christ's return.

This stereotypical image belies the Scriptural basis and significance of this movement. From a sociopolitical perspective, Zionism's roots stretch back to 1897 and the vision and leadership of Jewish Austro-Hungarian journalist Theodor Herzl. Within the church Zionism has progressively evolved for the last two thousand years, and there have been both vocal proponents and opponents of the movement throughout its history. After the death of the early apostles Israel's supporters within the church bravely demonstrated their support with prayer and action.

Unfortunately, from a historical perspective, they largely remained a minority. Not until the 1800s did Christian support for Israel and the Jewish community arise.

I see the term *Zionism* as referring to the belief that the Jewish people have a right to return to their homeland. Since early Jewish history this restoration to Zion has been synonymous with the Jews' return to Jerusalem. *Christian Zionism* refers to the church's support for this cause. Christian proponents of the Zionist movement also tend to believe strongly in the biblical mandate to bless Israel with moral and financial support and prayer.

Says author David Rausch: "Zionism has been aided in the nineteenth and twentieth centuries by 'Christian Zionists.' Because of their premillennial eschatology...evangelicals have been particularly supportive of the restoration of the Jewish people to Israel and Israel itself in the twentieth century."[1] At the core of this belief lies the assertion that Israel has a right to the ancient land because the God of the Bible gave the land to it. And the capital of that land is Jerusalem, the Jews' eternal, holy city. Its other passionate belief is that Israel—like any other country—has a right to defend itself from ongoing threats and attacks.

Granted, Christian Zionism has its share of critics. Some label it "a modern theological and political movement that embraces the most extreme ideological positions of Zionism, thereby becoming detrimental to a just peace with Palestine and Israel."[2] In a sermon titled "A Place for Israel," well-known British theologian John R. Stott remarked, "Now who, according to the New Testament perspective, is Israel today? And the answer we are going to see from the Bible is this extraordinary event—that true Israel today is neither Jews nor Israelis, but believers in the Messiah, even if they are gentiles."[3]

One leading misconception of Christian Zionists regards our motives. Supposedly we want to expedite the return of Jesus Christ. This falsehood is fueled by media twists and misinformation that are often circulated by secular observers. Writes David Brog, whom I quoted earlier, "The media have conjured up a more sinister motive behind Christian Zionism, and this false motive has been mentioned so often that it has taken root in the popular understanding of the phenomenon."[4]

With regard to the leading motivation of Christian Zionists being to hasten the Second Coming of Christ, nothing could be further from the truth. As Brog observes: "All of the leading Christian Zionists share this dispensationalist belief that man cannot alter God's timetable for the Second Coming."[5] In addition, author Elliott Abrams points out the irony of Christian Zionists' motives weighed against the widespread Jewish belief in a coming Messiah: "Many Jews argue that evangelicals favor Jewish control of the Holy Land because they see it as a step toward the messianic era when Jesus returns, and therefore as a means to an end inimical to Judaism."[6]

Pastor John Hagee, considered by many to be today's most forthright Christian Zionist in America, is founder and chairman of the aforementioned Christians United for Israel (CUFI). This ministry sprang up from a meeting of four hundred evangelicals in San Antonio, Texas, in 2006.

They gathered for the sole purpose of generating support for Israel and the Jewish community. Since then, CUFI has expanded to more than one million members across the United States and sponsors more than fifty pro-Israel events a month.

Concerning the moral obligation of Christians to support Israel, Hagee believes this aligns with God's will: "The Jewish people gave to us the patriarchs, Abraham, Isaac, and Jacob. The prophets Elijah, Daniel, Zechariah.... Every word in your Bible was written by Jewish hands. The first family of Christianity, Mary, Joseph, and Jesus, were Jewish. Jesus Christ, a Jewish rabbi from Nazareth, made this statement: 'Salvation is of the Jews.' The point is this: If you take away the Jewish contribution to Christianity, there would be no Christianity."[7]

Hagee traces his pro-Israel stance to the late 1970s, when he toured the Holy Land with a group from his church and returned a Zionist because—as he told *Weekly Standard* reporter Jennifer Rubin—"I felt the presence of God in the city of Jerusalem like no place on earth."[8] Hagee says CUFI provides pro-Israeli Christians and churches opportunities to express solidarity with Israel. During its annual conference in Washington DC every July, Hagee leads more than five thousand Christians to Capitol Hill. Rubin noted in her story: "When they lobby on Capitol Hill, [Hagee] said, his members 'ask the leadership of our government to stop putting pressure on Israel to divide Jerusalem and the land of Israel.'"[9]

Commitment to Scripture

To defeat the plagues of replacement theology and anti-Semitism, the church needs a rock-solid commitment to Scripture and biblical authority. The classical argument against replacement theology is found in Romans 11. There Paul constructs his most important argument regarding God's eternal placement and sustaining of Israel: "I ask then: Did God reject his people? By no means! I am an Israelite myself, a descendant of Abraham, from the tribe of Benjamin. God did not reject his people, whom he foreknew" (Rom. 11:1–2).

In this passage Paul reminded the Romans of two key truths: (1) he himself is a Jew, and (2) God has not rejected the Jews, nor has He replaced the Jews with the Christian church. With this in mind Paul uses the metaphor of an "olive tree" to depict to his audience the importance—and value—of Israeli and Gentile alike in sharing in God's grace. He also warns Gentiles to "not boast" (v. 18) or become "arrogant" (v. 20) because they, in fact, are the ones being "grafted" into the olive tree (v. 24). Bible scholar Marvin Wilson expounds: "Here Paul points to a unity between Israel (the tree) and the Gentiles (the engrafted branches) by drawing upon a horticulture metaphor familiar from the Old Testament. It is Hebraic through and through.... Thus the Church, firmly planted in Hebraic soil, finds its true identity in connection with Israel."[10]

Paul pointed out early in Romans 11: "So too, at the present time there is a remnant chosen by grace" (v. 5). He follows soon after with this statement: "Did they stumble so as to fall beyond recovery? Not at all! Rather, because of their transgression, salvation has come to the Gentiles to make Israel envious. But if their transgression means riches for the world, and their loss means riches for the Gentiles, how much greater riches will their fullness bring!" (vv. 11–12). Clearly for Paul this remnant is Israel, the people of God. Because the Jews have temporarily missed God's opportunity for salvation, their stumbling does not translate to an eternal fall.

Contrary to replacement theology, God has not rejected Israel—historically, ethnically, morally, or spiritually. However, by way of adoption He grafted in the Christian church. Jews have not been *cut off* or *cut out*; Gentiles have been *grafted in*. This opportunity came as an *addition to* God's kingdom rather than a *replacement of* Israel. Wilson adds: "Those in the Christian community who may feel the olive tree died about two thousand years ago and thus the root has no life now left in it must read Romans 11 again...there Paul emphatically says that God has not rejected his people...for God's gifts and his call are irrevocable (v. 29)....The common belief today that Gentiles have replaced the Jewish tree, rather than being grafted into it, is a position of post–New Testament Christian triumphalism that finds no support in Romans 11."[11]

Ever since Paul defended the Jews, the church has experienced battles over replacement theology and anti-Semitism. Nearly eighteen hundred years passed with little support for Christian Zionism until the leadership and influence of John Nelson Darby. Despite his cessationist views—which I obviously do not agree with—this nineteenth-century Anglo-Irish evangelist opposed replacement theology and voiced strong support for Israel. Thanks to his influence, years later members of the Plymouth Brethren (also known as "Darbyites") demonstrated commitment and support for Jewish people during World War II in the village of Vichy, France. Wilson agrees: "What made the Plymouth Brethren unique was not their views on the church but their views on the Jews. The Brethren rejected replacement theology and instead embraced a theology that held that the Jews were still the 'Israel' to which so much is promised in the Bible."[12]

From Darby's influence in the mid-1800s sprang other notable Zionists. Moody Bible Institute founder D. L. Moody and theologian C. I. Scofield, whose noted study Bible remains popular today, followed in the late 1800s. The dispensationalist movement of the latter 1900s, featuring such spokesmen as Hal Lindsey, Tim LaHaye, and Jerry Falwell, has its roots in Darby's approach. The theology of dispensationalism and fundamentalism they supported proved conducive to standing with Israel by influencing mainstream Christianity.

Dispensationalism prepared the way for Christian Zionism, with its core conviction that Jews were legal heirs to the land of Israel. According to Bible scholar and pastor Paul Enns, fundamentalism carried the convictions that "stood for the historic doctrines of the Christian faith in contrast to modern religious liberals, who rejected doctrines such as the inspiration of Scripture, the deity of Christ, and the genuineness of miracles."[13]

Fundamentalists embraced the inerrancy and authority of Scripture, especially the idea of modern-day Jews as God's chosen people. As Enns says, "In the early years of [the twentieth] century, fundamentalism had a good record in defending orthodoxy. The intellectual giants of orthodoxy as well as the prominent preachers of that day stood for the historic Christian faith. These leaders defended the doctrines that have been believed by devout Christians throughout the centuries."[14]

However, not until the middle to late 1900s did major and mainline denominations start rejecting replacement theology and demonstrate support for Israel. According to Elliott Abrams, the Evangelical Lutheran Church in Germany (1950), the Catholic Church (1965), the United Methodist Church (1972), and the Presbyterian Church USA (1987) finally refuted this "supersessionism" teaching, proclaiming that God had not broken His covenant with Israel, nor had the church replaced the Jewish people. The United Church of Christ (1987) and the Disciples of Christ (1993) followed suit by decreeing the legitimacy of Israel and that through God's grace, the Jewish people remain God's chosen people.[15]

Today many Christian Zionist churches and organizations firmly espouse Israel's right to its ancient homeland, whose capital is Jerusalem (Gen. 13:15; 15:18; 17:7–8). This is the Promised Land that God gave it. Rather than an occupier of the land, Israel owns the land. Christian Zionists—including many in the African American church—believe that Israel has the right to protect its borders and defend itself against ongoing, violent threats and attacks. Promoting such support for Israel are grassroots organizations such as CUFI, the International Fellowship of Christians and Jews, the International Christian Embassy, Eagles' Wings, and the Center for Jewish-Christian Understanding and Cooperation (CJCUC), whose objective is to provide a vehicle through which pro-Israel churches, parachurch organizations, ministries, and individuals can speak with one voice.

Unfortunately there are still far too many today (including some Christians) who oppose Israel and maintain the anti-Semitic principles of the past. This is tragic, since this was the climate in which replacement theology once thrived. It started with the idea that when the Jews rejected Jesus as Messiah, the church replaced them as the beneficiaries of God's Abrahamic covenant (as if God had somehow forgotten His ancient promise). This led to the view that the church had become Abraham's spiritual descendants and thus represented the "new" Israel. The church's theology was soon reflected in its actions.

This perspective, rooted in contempt for Israel, led to the exclusion of Israel in terms of theological reflection and consideration. Ronald Diprose, academic dean at the Italian Bible Institute in Rome, writes, "In spite of the fact that Israel's status as an elect people is confirmed by Paul in Romans 9–11, the view that the church had completely replaced Israel in God's plan became the dominant opinion in post-Apostolic Christendom.... Some church fathers went further when they affirmed that the Church had always been the true Israel of which the physical Israelites were but one visible sign."[16]

The Post-Apostolic Period

Many of Israel's opponents arose during the post-apostolic period, including such popular leaders as Justin Martyr, St. Augustine, John Chrysostom, and Martin Luther. These classical, well-versed theologians unfortunately contributed to this errant theology through their anti-Israeli writings. In *Standing With Israel* Brog quotes from Martyr's *Dialogue With Trypho*: "We [Christians] have been led to God through this crucified Christ, and we are the true spiritual Israel, and the descendants of Judah, Jacob, Isaac, and Abraham, who, though uncircumcised, was approved and blessed by God because of his faith and was called the father of many nations."[17]

Speaking of the Jews, St. John Chrysostom (bishop of Antioch) declared, "Through your madness against Christ you have committed the ultimate transgression. This is why you are being punished now worse than in the past.... If this were not the case God would not have turned his back on you so completely.... It is because you killed Christ. It is because you stretched out your hand against the Lord. It is because you shed the precious blood that there is now no restoration, no mercy anymore and no defense."[18]

St. Augustine, whose early church views would hold sway for years, wrote: "For if they lived with that testimony of the Scriptures only in their own land, and not everywhere, the obvious result would be that the Church, which is everywhere, would not have them available among all nations as witness to the prophecies which were given beforehand concerning Christ."[19]

Anti-Semitism and Jewish persecution continued long after those early days of the church. From the Crusaders of the eleventh century to the Spanish Inquisition in the late 1400s, the historical considerations of non-support for Israel were obvious and determined. Says scholar Lance Lambert: "The story has many faces with many moods. Sometimes it is the story of bloody persecution and violent hatred, as in the period of the Crusaders in the 11th–12th centuries, or the Inquisition in the 15th and 16th centuries, or of the pogroms in the late 19th and early 20th centuries, or the Nazi era of the 1930s and '40s."[20]

The year 1215 saw another significant development that would later promote Jewish persecution. The Fourth Lateran Council, a gathering of more than one thousand church leaders, determined numerous policies, including the official relationship between Christians and Jews in terms of church polity and expectations. John Hagee writes of this meeting: "It would be the officially approved standard of conduct for European Christians toward Jews through the centuries and was still in place when Adolf Hitler eventually came to power."[21]

Of particular significance is that this council gave rise to the marked separation between Jews and non-Jews in Europe that would bear treacherous fruit seven centuries later. The council did so by dictating that Jews wear separate clothing to distinguish themselves from Christians. According to noted church historian Norman P. Tanner, the council decreed: "In order that the offence of such a damnable mixing may not spread further, under the excuse of a mistake of this kind, we decree that such persons of either sex, in every Christian province and at all times, are to be distinguished in public from other people by the character of their dress—seeing moreover that this was enjoined upon them by Moses himself, as we read."[22] This distinctive clothing decree would survive into the post-Reformation period four hundred years later, and eventually the yellow badge and Star of David would provide Hitler with the imagery to mark the Jews for abuse and execution.

Sadly, Martin Luther—the priest who helped spark the Reformation with his opposition to certain Catholic Church practices—would also serve as a leading source for Hitler's anti-Semitic mania. Luther's writings also provided theological cover for the mad dictator, who proclaimed himself a devout Christian even as he unleashed the Holocaust. During the Reformation period Luther quickly rose as one of the most demonstrative opponents of Israel. In his work *On the Jews and Their Lies*, Luther openly condemned the Jews: "First, their synagogues or churches should be set on fire....Second, their homes should be broken down and destroyed....Third, they should be deprived of their prayer books and Talmuds in which such idolatry, lies, cursing and blasphemy are taught....Fourthly, their rabbis must be forbidden under threat of death to teach anymore."[23]

Despite separating from the Catholic Church, Luther would influence many Catholics as well as Protestants with his embrace of replacement theology. Tragically the

church became one of the sinister hands behind the Holocaust. In addition to churches in Europe who overtly or
covertly supported Jewish persecution stood the legions of
silent Catholics and Protestants in America.

Thanks to the influence of Martin Luther in the 1500s
and stretching forward to the Roman Catholic Church
in the 1940s, the post-Reformation period has seen considerable opposition to the Jewish people. Many mainline or liberal denominational churches have opposed
Israel's statehood, while the tentacles of replacement
theology spread around numerous American Christian
leaders. Diprose says this "failure to reflect seriously on
Israel in light of all the relevant biblical data has serious
consequences for the entire enterprise of Christian theology."[24] Sadly, much of the lack of support for Israel feels
like racism in modern America. Its covert existence is
expressed through the philosophical tenet that with the
church as the new children of promise, we have no need
for an ethnic, literal Israel.

Modern-day "watchmen" on the wall—such as John
Hagee and David Brog of CUFI—see such a belief as a
destructive ideology. It aims to destroy Israel with the
same efficiency Iran's Islamic rulers would use if it were
possible to accomplish their goal. Because replacement
theology has advanced among many church leaders and
laypersons, the church must strive to dispel this errant
ideology—and be on guard against the ongoing influence of anti-Semitism, particularly in the pews. Says
Hagee: "As Christians we should ask God's forgiveness
and ask the Jewish people for forgiveness of every act of

anti-Semitism in our past. The Crusades. The Spanish Inquisition. Martin Luther's 'Concerning the Jews and Their Lies.' The Final Solution of Adolf Hitler, which was carried out by baptized Christians in good standing with their church."[25]

To defeat replacement theology and the anti-Semitism that drives it, the church must implement determined, intentional practices. Educating members about the biblical and theological support for Israel from Old and New Testament alike is essential in African American churches. Equipping the local church with relevant, contemporary information to combat replacement theology will strengthen support for Israel. I believe today's African American church can create a unique opportunity to stand with those who were so key to the advancement of civil rights in the 1950s and 1960s—and play a major role in influencing modern culture.

Chapter 3

EDUCATING
OTHERS

W HEN IT COMES to standing for Israel, few contemporary Christian Zionists and theologians stand
taller than Dietrich Bonhoeffer. This German pastor,
anti-Nazi activist, and outspoken author bravely risked
his life to fight Hitler and the Nazi regime while challenging an apathetic church. His 1937 book *The Cost of
Discipleship* is considered a modern classic. More recently
a 2010 biography of Bonhoeffer by Eric Metaxas became
a surprise best seller, awakening a new generation to the
significance of this hero of the faith.

Less than a month before Germany surrendered to
Allied forces this Lutheran minister died at the end of a
noose while imprisoned at a Nazi concentration camp. Yet
his legacy and impact live on, affecting the entire Christian world from the post–World War II era until today.
Noted Bible professor Walter Elwell writes of Bonhoeffer:
"At that time he had not attained the international recognition and fame that have been accorded him since the
1950s. It was after the posthumous publication and translation of his *Letters and Papers From Prison* (first released

in 1951) that Bonhoeffer came to the attention of Christendom throughout the world."[1]

Men like Bonhoeffer, American theologian Reinhold Niebuhr, and Swiss theologian Karl Barth all lived during an era when Israel and the Jewish people desperately needed the church's support. These three brave men are sparkling examples for modern-day Christians, standing as they do at the crossroads of Christian Zionism and education. Moral conscience and determined activism will make a lasting difference to the Jewish people. Generating support for Israel in the twenty-first century will require an ongoing emphasis on education and activism, starting in pulpits and moving through the pews.

To appreciate more fully the genesis of Bonhoeffer's development from a lukewarm believer into an outspoken leader, consider his history. Growing up in Berlin in a conservative family, in his youth he seldom visited or attended church. Even after becoming a theologian and minister, he demonstrated limited church involvement. Consequently Bonhoeffer had little understanding of church as community or the faith to prompt undertaking social change.

Ironically the 1930s' era African American church helped awaken Bonhoeffer to social and political struggles from a Christian perspective. He came to this understanding during a teaching fellowship at Union Theological Seminary in New York. Historian Henry Mitchell notes: "The black pulpit had social consciousness...so here was a man of considerable intelligence and training...a man of real passion, solid biblical commitment, who was also involved in social and political issues of his time."[2]

Under Niebuhr's teaching at Union, Bonhoeffer gained much of his appetite for social activism and engagement from the teachings and literature of black writers and preachers. The black church's social struggles helped him understand the worth and value of the church as a community of social change. Niebuhr, considered the father of social ethics in the United States, enlightened his protégé to the potential of the church's influence on social ills.

Author Josiah Young notes that Bonhoeffer's political activity during the war (particularly his opposition to white supremacists) bears a strong relationship to his friendship with African Americans: "Bonhoeffer spent much of this time in Harlem while he studied at Union. Frank Fisher, an African American Union student and one of Bonhoeffer's closest friends during his stay in New York City, introduced Bonhoeffer to Harlem and to the Abyssinian Baptist Church. Bonhoeffer attended the church most Sundays during the time he studied at Union."[3] In time it became clear that, as theologian Geffrey Kelly notes, "the purpose of theology [for Bonhoeffer] was to change this world for the better."[4]

Challenging Churches to Stand

Amid the mounting anti-Semitism of the 1930s, Bonhoeffer challenged hundreds of pastors and churches to stand with the Jews, especially during a speech he titled "The Church and the Jewish Question." Noted professor John De Gruchy says of Bonhoeffer, "We can say that Dietrich Bonhoeffer was the first German evangelical theologian to make a statement that the church couldn't stand by and let this happen without doing something about it."[5] Bonhoeffer's growing emphasis on the person of Jesus would not permit him to side with a German church that placed a higher value on nationalism than faith in Christ.

Bonhoeffer had a special relationship with Barth. Both men were leaders in the Confessing Church, which arose in 1933 and the following year issued the Barmen Declaration, with Barth as its chief author. This statement opposed the Nazi-supported "German Christian" movement and objected to the church becoming subordinate to the state. Coinciding with Adolf Hitler's rise to power, the Confessing Church would serve as a thorn in Hitler's side throughout World War II. It courageously opposed the diabolical dictator's schemes, which he often cleverly disguised in a "Christian" cloak, even though in reality they never resembled authentic Christianity. De Gruchy says, "The first struggle was around the question of the churches' freedom to preach the Gospel, not about the Jewish question...but then gradually Bonhoeffer recognized that the real question is not the freedom of the church preaching the gospel...the real issue is the church standing by its victims."[6]

Bonhoeffer questioned the church's seeming apathy and silence during the beginning of the Holocaust. In a letter to Barth in September 1933, Bonhoeffer said: "In your booklet (*Theologische Existenz heute*) you said that where a church adopted the Aryan paragraphs it would cease to be a Christian church. A considerable number of pastors here would agree with you in this view. Now the expected has happened, and I am therefore asking you on behalf of many friends, pastors and students, to let us know whether you feel that it is possible either to remain in a church which has ceased to be a Christian church or to continue to exercise a ministry which has become a privilege for Aryans."[7]

Many regard Bonhoeffer's influential professor, Niebuhr, as one of the leading North American theologians and political philosophers of the twentieth century. During the 1930s and 1940s Niebuhr's thoughts were paramount in defending Israel and the Jewish community. As I mentioned, Niebuhr was considered the father of social ethics, a status stemming from his impact on Bonhoeffer and other influential figures. Christian ethics professor Ronald Stone says of Niebuhr, "He was not primarily a pastor or a preacher. He was not primarily an adviser to public figures. He was not primarily an author of immense productivity. He was first and foremost a professor of Protestant social ethics in the context of Protestant theological education."[8]

Niebuhr tried to awaken Americans to the horrors of German anti-Semitism before it led to the Holocaust. Along with ally Paul Tillich, Niebuhr formed Christian organizations to aid Israel and the Jewish community. Niebuhr also served on the executive committee of the Christian Council on Palestine, a pro-Jewish-homeland organization. Stone writes: "Niebuhr, along with Tillich, came to a position that may be regarded as Christian Zionism. They passionately believed in the need for U.S. support for a secure homeland for the Jews, and they believed Palestine to be the best and historically determined site."[9]

Though in full support of Israel and the Jewish people, as a true champion for justice for all people Niebuhr also supported Palestinian Arabs. Says Stone: "He [Niebuhr] noted that injury was done to the Arabs, but still he wrote, 'Many Christians are pro-Zionist in the sense that they believe a homeless people require a homeland.' Justice still required, in Niebuhr's understanding, further work on behalf of the Palestinians."[10] Unlike many of his contemporaries, Niebuhr sought to assist both sides of the struggle between Israel and the Palestinian people. Just as Niebuhr did not devote unswerving loyalty to the Jewish call, he believed that the "new" Israel would not be a world power based on geographical or political might. Instead, he saw it as a place of service, a la Mark 10:45: "For even the Son of Man did not come to be served, but to serve, and to give his life as a ransom for many."

A Strong Supporter of Israel

During Hitler's rise to ultimate power Barth didn't spare criticism of the "German Christian" movement that purported to see the hand of God at work through Nazism. Barth's famous pamphlet, *Theological Existence Today*, represented a manifesto for Protestant opposition to Hitler's regime. The Barmen Declaration achieved equal importance through its affirmation of the Lordship of Jesus Christ in the face of powerful Nazi opposition.

During this time Barth wrote, "Jesus Christ, as he is attested to us in Holy Scripture, is the one Word of God

whom we have to hear, and whom we have to trust and
obey in life and in death. We reject the false doctrine
that the church could and should recognize as a source
of its proclamation, beyond and beside this one Word of
God, yet, other event, powers, historic figures, and truths
as God's revelation."[11] When an oath of loyalty to Hitler
became mandatory for all civil servants in 1935—including
Barth as a university professor—he refused to sign. His
Nazi bosses dismissed him from his teaching post and
banned him from public speaking.

Despite this anti-Nazi stance, Barth believed that
while the Christian church had a responsibility to speak
against social injustice, it should avoid excessive political
entanglements. He wrote, "The church is in movement
when making confession. To many present-day questions
it can and must be silent with its yes and no, perhaps pro-
visionally, perhaps again as time and possibility change. It
must be silent when it finds no place to bear real witness
to Jesus Christ, when it cannot present a yes or no that
carries this witness....But woe to the church if when the
time does come it is silent, or merely reflects or discusses,
or retreats into mere recitation. Woe to it if it sleeps, not
just when great things are happening in the world...but
when Jesus Christ himself is under assault and we ought
to be watching with him."[12]

Barth thought the church needed both social and
spiritual motives to defend Israel and the Jewish community. At a 1954 seminar titled "Christ the Hope of the
World," Barth said, "We must first speak about the people
who in its hope rests on the same subject as is the basis

of our hope, the coming of the Messiah. This people is Israel. For three thousand years it has had a history that cannot be compared with that of any other people. After a brief ascendancy, it has trodden a path of suffering that is marked outwardly by war, defeat, captivity, suppression, dispersal, need, misery, and the most cruel persecution. Yet it will not and cannot perish until that hope is demonstrably fulfilled for it."[13]

In the days when the president of Iran openly advocates the destruction of Israel, it is interesting to note Barth's belief that Israel could not idly stand by and wait for other governmental, social or civic groups, or other associations to speak out on its behalf. Only the church can be a divine beacon of hope in leading the cause in supporting Israel. I agree with Barth that it is readily understood that the hope of Israel as a lasting nation is contingent on the church courageously acting as it should. As Barth said, "That hope is by nature different from hopes that rely on immanent processes or human programs. It is grounded in the promise God gave his chosen people. The content of this promise is that God will set up his kingdom on earth."[14]

Theologically Barth was widely recognized for his insightful contribution concerning the "election" of Israel and the church. He insisted that God manifested Himself in both roles as the God of Old Testament Israel and the God of New Testament grace—with that grace found in Jesus Christ. Theology professor Joseph Mangina writes, "In the Old Testament 'election' means 'Israel,' since God does not exist without his people. In the New Testament this same language is applied to the church, the *ekklesia* chosen 'in him [Christ] before the foundation of the world' (Eph. 1:4). God's election takes up space in the world through the existence of these peoples. Or should we say this people: in a decisive stroke. Barth construes Israel and this church as but two forms of a single community, centered in Christ.... The God of the Law and the Prophets is already the God of grace, just as Jesus Christ is unintelligible apart from the promises given to Israel. As he reads the Bible, Barth simply finds it impossible to narrate God's identity apart from that of Israel."[15]

The Role of Education

I am a firm believer that the most effective way of building support for Israel and the Jewish people is through comprehensive education. How vital is this? Educating people in the local church can play an integral role in increasing knowledge in multiple settings, as those who learn then share their insights with others. In the Christian tradition the Bible reinforces the idea of educating those in the church. As the Old Testament prophet Hosea wrote, "My people are destroyed for lack of knowledge" (Hosea 4:6, NKJV). In the New Testament Jesus became the chief role model of teaching: "Jesus went through all the towns and villages, teaching in their synagogues, preaching the good news of the kingdom and healing every disease and sickness" (Matt. 9:35). The physician Luke also records: "Then he [Jesus] opened their minds so they could understand the Scriptures" (Luke 24:45).

Not only did Jesus educate the people in the first century, but also He expects the church to do the same today.

That is seen through what we know as the Great Commission: "Therefore go and make disciples of all nations, baptizing them in the name of the Father and of the Son and of the Holy Spirit, and teaching them to obey everything I have commanded you. And surely I am with you always, to the very end of the age" (Matt. 28:19–20). The apostle Paul continued this emphasis on adult education by acknowledging teaching as a spiritual gift. His letter to the Romans includes this statement: "Having gifts that differ according to the grace given to us, let us use them: if prophecy, in proportion to our faith; if service, in our serving; *he who teaches, in his teaching*" (Rom. 12:6–7, RSV, emphasis added). Paul continued this theme in 2 Timothy: "And the things you have heard me say in the presence of many witnesses entrust to reliable men who will also be qualified to teach others" (2 Tim. 2:2).

The ultimate objective of education is to empower and equip Christians to fulfill the will of God for their personal lives and ministry and to fulfill the expectations of God's kingdom. The African American church must stand with Israel. To do so, it must approach the task of educating its members about God's lasting covenant with His chosen people with determination and an intentional focus.

Recently I conducted a series of educational seminars at our church. In addition to teaching about Israel, I wanted to learn more about the level of knowledge and understanding of participants about the Jewish people. These seminars included a review of Old and New Testament references to the Jewish people and the personal and moral motives for supporting Israel. The lessons included one that dealt with the discovering of the importance of Jewish and African American relationships, most notably during the civil rights era. I also discussed some of the contributions to the Jewish community the late Dr. Martin Luther King Jr. made.

As a result of these seminars, participants could more fully grasp the biblical, theological, and moral motivations for the church—especially in the African American community—to embrace Israel. I believe we accomplished our intended goal by successfully increasing the knowledge of church members and others. Many expressed a desire to engage in future studies on this topic. The question-and-answer segments after each session revealed a genuine desire to continue dialogue and discussions and make this curriculum an annual emphasis. Some members suggested starting small groups and additional Bible studies concerning the African American church's involvement with the Jewish people.

From this experience and discussions with other pastors from various regions I have concluded that comprehensive education can create a strong system of support and solidarity among African American churches and communities nationwide. Educating members is essential to our churches and the Jewish community as we seek to build bridges of commonality and cultural appreciation. It is my hope that African American church overtures will strengthen and encourage Israel—proving invaluable and sustaining in her current hour of need.

In chapter 1 I briefly mentioned Dr. Marvin Wilson in

quoting an excerpt from his book *Our Father Abraham*. This work provides additional reasons education and instruction are keys to strengthening support for Israel and the Jewish community. It emphasizes several ways of reaching out to other Christians, including understanding theological themes and scriptures. Among those Wilson references:

- Galatians 3:29: "If you belong to Christ, then you are Abraham's seed, and heirs according to the promise."

- Acts 8:34–35: "The eunuch asked Philip, 'Tell me, please, who is the prophet talking about, himself or someone else?' Then Philip began with that very passage of Scripture and told him the good news about Jesus."

For Wilson, Christianity started with Abraham surrendering before God then extended to Gentiles through faith in Christ. He affirms in his writings the necessity of Christian support for Israel and the Jewish community but includes several important considerations:

1. Christian support for Israel cannot equate to an anti-Palestinian mind-set. Wilson writes, "Christian solidarity with Israel does not imply the negation of Palestinian Arabs. This is not an 'us or them,' 'right or wrong' issue."[16] He goes on to say that Palestinian Arab Christians are also beneficiaries of

the Jewish spiritual heritage, and they are
as indebted to the Jews as American and
European believers. Wilson reminds us
that the Old and New Testaments contain
"renewed" covenants originally given to the
Jewish people.

2. Christian support must never succumb
   to the attitude that if one criticizes Israel
   or objects to its policies, he opposes God.
   Wilson writes, "People are not necessarily
   anti-Semitic or anti-Zionist if they oppose
   certain Israeli political policies or military
   actions. At times, we may need to express
   our strongest disapproval of the one whom
   we care about most deeply and love the
   most."[17]

3. Christian support for Israel must not place
   the Jewish people on a pedestal, which
   in turn creates unrealistic expectations
   or inaccurate images of Israel. He writes,
   "Sometimes this idealization has led Christians to turn against the Jewish community because their expectations have not
   been met. Christian friendship and concern
   shown to Jews—as to all people—must
   always be unconditional, not founded on
   prerequisites or any preconceived checklist
   of virtues."[18]

4. Christian support for Israel must not include imposing one's specific political views, religious beliefs, or personal agendas upon the Jewish people. According to Wilson, "The question of timing is always significant in the way God works. It is easy to become impatient with the slowness of peace talks or the bent toward secularism in much of contemporary Israeli society. God's sense of timing in accomplishing his purposes in history is often different from that of human beings."[19]

This latter topic often prompts questions about salvation for the Jews. Like Wilson I believe that everything is in God's sovereign timing and plans for Israel—including salvation and redemption. Isaiah 55:9 reminds us, "As the heavens are higher than the earth, so are my ways higher than your ways and my thoughts than your thoughts." Thus I can appreciate that my convictions concerning salvation and redemption of the Jews are God's responsibility—not mine. As a Christian my duty is to pray and show sincere kindness and love to our Jewish brothers and sisters.

Though this viewpoint brings much criticism from mainline churches and sometimes even messianic Jewish groups, in 1 Corinthians Paul supplies an illustration of the role of Christians: "What, after all, is Apollos? And what is Paul? Only servants, through whom you came to believe—as the Lord has assigned to each his task. I planted the seed, Apollos watered it, but God made it grow. So neither he who plants nor he who waters is anything, but only God, who makes things grow" (1 Cor. 3:5–7).

Perhaps the greatest contribution of Wilson's writings stems from his caution for us as Christians to avoid becoming too cerebral or theoretical about Israel, particularly as it relates to the latter days and the end times. He believes that there is a mystical paradox about Israel that both Christians and Jews are still trying to understand. God is sovereign in His plans and timing. Until the Second Coming we must strive to remain faithful to supporting the people who still bear God's original promise.

Chapter 4

THE ROLE OF THE AFRICAN AMERICAN CHURCH

THEN HAGGAI, THE LORD's messenger, gave this message of the LORD to the people: 'I am with you,' declares the LORD. So the LORD stirred up the spirit of Zerubbabel son of Shealtiel, governor of Judah, and the spirit of Joshua son of Jehozadak, the high priest, and the spirit of the whole remnant of the people. They came and began to work..." (Hag. 1:13–14). I could sense palpable excitement filling the auditorium at one of the numerous "A Night to Honor Israel" events sponsored during the year by Christians United for Israel. Shouts of joy, tears, and passion arose from the crowd of more than three thousand who had flocked to the megachurch hosting the rally. Choking back tears at the raw emotion this display stirred within me, I thought, "One hasn't really experienced the 'shock and awe' of the amazement of a pro-Israel solidarity event until they attend one hosted by an African American church!"

Indeed, I challenge you to avoid similar sensations if you ever have the privilege of witnessing sincere love and support shared in such a setting—particularly when it is accompanied by high praises to the Lord, loving expressions, and looks of deep appreciation from the Jewish people in attendance. Many Jewish friends have expressed to me that they never thought they would live to see the day when Jews and Christians would stand shoulder to shoulder in unity and solidarity—particularly in an African American church.

Nor is the experience I enjoyed an isolated incident. I sense a "stirring in the Spirit" among African American churches to support Israel and the Jewish community! From coast to coast and church to church I see a passionate, prophetic stirring from the Lord to intercede for Israel. I believe my brothers and sisters will arise to act as the same kind of bold voice the Jews offered for us during the civil rights era. I am humbled and honored to play a small role in such a historically significant development. I love watching these cultural bridges arising and extending unwavering support to the people of Israel.

Despite the nay-saying rhetoric of some critics from within and outside our congregations, the African American church is not dead. On the contrary, it is alive and well! The possibilities of support and strength that the African American church can provide to the Jewish community are boundless. One can only imagine what could be accomplished if these two communities partnered for the same cause. Our Jewish brethren can draw comfort from the strong support for the God of Abraham, Isaac, and Jacob that exists in the African American church— and, by extension, for the children of the divine promise in Genesis 12:1–3.

This isn't some kind of idle promise, either. According

to the Pew Forum on Religion and Public Life, when compared to other ethnicities in the United States, African Americans are significantly more religious on a variety of spiritual measures. African Americans are more likely to have an absolute belief in God, pray more, interpret biblical scriptures as literal, and attend worship services than their non–African American counterparts. Nearly eight in ten (79 percent) affirm that religion is very important in their daily lives, compared to 56 percent of all adults.[1]

In comments included with the survey, the author said: "While the U.S. is generally considered a highly religious nation, African-Americans are markedly more religious on a variety of measures than the U.S. population as a whole, including level of affiliation with a religion, attendance at religious services, frequency of prayer and religion's importance in life."[2] While just 39 percent of all Americans report attending religious services at least once a week, a majority of African Americans (53 percent) report the same. Similarly, while 58 percent of all Americans report praying at least once a day, a significantly higher number of African Americans (76 percent) report such behavior.[3]

When it comes to core spiritual beliefs, African Americans express higher levels of core spiritual beliefs than other Americans too. They are more likely to believe in God with absolute certainly (88 percent, as compared to 71 percent of the total adult population) and interpret Scripture as the literal word of God (55 percent vs. 33 percent.) Interestingly African Americans show comfort with religion's role in social matters and politics, which is good news when it comes to support for Israel. According to the same survey, more than six in ten African Americans (61 percent) say houses of worship should express their views on social and political matters, while only 36 percent say churches should avoid these topics.[4] These facts—and many others—stem from the direct impact and influence of the church.[5]

The Established Foundation

Jesus Christ called the church to be the established foundation of the community. The Gospel of Matthew includes this ringing declaration Jesus made to Peter: "And I tell you, you are Peter, and on this rock I will build my church, and the powers of death shall not prevail against it. I will give you the keys of the kingdom of heaven, and whatever you bind on earth shall be bound in heaven, and whatever you loose on earth shall be loosed in heaven" (Matt. 16:18–19, RSV).

Paul told one of the first churches ever formed that its primary functions unfold through its designated and appointed leaders: "And in the church God has appointed first of all apostles, second prophets, third teachers, then workers of miracles, also those having gifts of healing, those able to help others, those with gifts of administration, and those speaking in different kinds of tongues" (1 Cor. 12:28). The church remains the fundamental anchor of conviction and truth.

The African American church has existed for more than four hundred years on this continent, arising long before the formation of the United States. Understanding its unique, distinctive qualities includes grasping its core objectives and painful history. The late C. Eric Lincoln, a noted professor and author who first picked cotton at the age of thirteen to help support his family, wrote that the "complexities of black churches as social institutions require a more dynamic and interactional theoretical perspective because they have played more complex roles and assumed more comprehensive burdens in their communities than is true of most white and ethic churches."[6]

For centuries the bedrock of the black community, the African American church earned this position because of its leading role as the driving force for liberation and freedom of our once-enslaved people. Says Lincoln: "As the only stable and coherent institutional area to emerge from slavery, black churches were not only dominant in their communities but they also became the womb of black culture and a number of major social institutions."[7]

The perspectives of Lincoln and notable African American theologian and historian James Cone offer insights into the identity, contributions, and distinctives of the African American church and its theology. In the book he coauthored with Lawrence H. Mamiya, *The Black Church in the African American Experience*, Lincoln wrote that theoretical assumptions underlie assessments and evaluation of the African American church: "The religious dimension of black churches is found in the black sacred cosmos, a unique Afro-Christian worldview that was forged among black people from both the African and Euro-American traditions during the eighteenth and nineteenth centuries. The black sacred cosmos permeated all of the social institutions and cultural traditions of black people."[8] He said of its unique culture: "While the general structure of beliefs, rituals, and organization of black church remained the same as white churches, black Christians often gave different nuances and emphases to their theological views."[9] These comments symbolize the importance of the shared struggle and pleas for deliverance that affect both African American and Jewish culture.

Cone also offers a fascinating view of the unique theological traditions of the African American church: "Black theologians and preachers have rejected the white church's attempt to separate love from justice and religion from politics because we are proud descendants of a black religious tradition that has always interpreted its confession of faith according to the people's commitment to the struggle for earthly freedom."[10] For Cone this had more to do with social and political struggle, characterized by deliverance and freedom, than the views expressed in traditional Western and European theology.

Despite the shorter tenure of black theology—when measured against a two-thousand-year Eurocentric history—it is still vital to grasp these differences. This theology will assume increasing importance in standing with Israel. Because of the black church's quest for liberation and freedom, our platform has the potential to offer great advantages to the Jewish community. The historical, shared experiences of dislocation, disenfranchisement, and disheartenment of both groups can forge aggressive and ambitious bonds for social change and improvement.

As social ethicist Peter Paris acknowledges, "The

growth of the black churches is both significant and inspirational. In its history lie the stories of countless men and women, often slaves and runaway slaves, frequently freed men of humble economic stature, completely lacking in social status."[11] Comments historian and professor James Eckman of the significance of these contributions: "The Black church in America had its origins in the slave religion of the American South. Deprived of their identity, oppressed by their masters, and unable to establish their own institutions, many slaves turned to Christianity. Faith in Jesus Christ gave them hope for the future when His justice would right the wrongs done to them."[12]

Contributing to the Community

Over the last several centuries the African American church has made significant contributions to the black community at large. Its impact and influence are unprecedented, especially during the peak of the civil rights movement. Just as for years the Jewish community experienced the tragic horrors that culminated in the Holocaust, during the century after the Civil War African Americans experienced humiliating racism, segregation, and disenfranchisement. Such mistreatment culminated in the African American church serving as the community's command center and lighthouse of hope and healing during the 1950s and 1960s.

Eckman agrees: "The modern civil rights movement largely grew out of the Black church. Leaders such as Dr. Martin Luther King, Jr., were themselves Baptist preachers who believed that the Bible condemned discrimination and racism. King, the undisputed leader of the nonviolent civil rights movement, organized African Americans and whites to pursue justice for all Americans regardless of race. Using the Bible and nonviolence, the movement impacted all aspects of American society."[13] Paris adds: "Historically, the churches have performed the many and varied functions of governance within the black community. The importance of those functions cannot be overemphasized. Constrained in every dimension of their common life by the dehumanizing conditions of white racism, blacks made their churches agencies for teaching the race how to respond to racial hostility in creative and constructive ways."[14]

Such comments provide a deeper realization of the potential of the black church's position and influence in regard to generating additional support during Israel's critical hour. For the African American church the vision of the gospel is to stand for that which is biblically right— and to do so even in the face of doctrinal opposition, adversity, and biblically uninformed criticism. (After all, those who don't know the Bible have no understanding of Israel's claim to its historic home.)

Not only did the African American church play a significant role during the civil rights era, its foremost leader stands as one of the most notable Christian Zionists of recent years. Between 1945 and 1968—the year an assassin struck him dead in Memphis—Dr. Martin Luther King Jr. became the "symbolic, mythic figure of that era."[15] The movement he spearheaded produced a lasting impact among African American churches involved in the struggle throughout the South. Not only was he a pioneering leader and influencer in advancing the rights of African Americans, but Dr. King also believed in supporting the Jewish community as well.

Unfortunately not all leaders and people in African American churches and communities shared King's values. In a speech titled "Social Justice and the Emerging New Age" at Western Michigan University in 1963, King commented, "I must admit that I have gone through those moments when I was greatly disappointed with the church and what it has done in this period of social change."[16] King believed it was the church's role and responsibility to bravely stand for social and ethical causes in the community. In his eyes it had a biblical mandate to speak up about social issues that affected all people—not just African Americans. In his speech "Strength to Love" King said, "Christians are bound to recognize any passionate concern for social justice....The Gospels abound with expressions of concern for the welfare of the poor...Christians are also bound to recognize the ideal of a world unity in which all barriers of caste and color are abolished. Christianity repudiates racism."[17]

King: Christian Zionist

While King devoted most of his life to the civil and equal rights of African Americans, King is also widely known for his leadership and influence for the Jewish cause and concern. In his book *Israel's Defense Line*, author I. L. Kenen noted that Dr. King said, "Peace for Israel means security, and we must stand with all our might to protect her right to exist, its territorial integrity and the right to use whatever sea lanes it needs. Israel is one of the great outposts of democracy in the world, and a marvelous example of what can be done, how desert land can be transformed into an oasis of brotherhood and democracy. Peace for Israel means security, and that security must be a reality."[18]

Observed sociology professor Jonathan Rieder: "King's solicitousness extended to Jewish audiences as well.... King underscored the collective interest served by protecting every minority in his 1958 address to the American Jewish Congress, [saying], 'My people were brought to American in chains. Your people were driven here to escape the chains fashioned for them in Europe. Our unity is born of our common struggle for centuries, not only to rid ourselves of bondage, but to make oppression of any people by others an impossibility.'"[19]

This may prompt the question: Was King a true Christian Zionist who held Israel and the Jewish community in a special place in his heart and theology? Or was he simply a global humanitarian and socially conscientious leader? I believe history supports the Zionist interpretation. Much of King's influence and inspiration came from the Jewish community's bouts with injustice, racism, and persecution. In 1968 King summed up the words of Rabbi Joachim Prinz's speech at the March on Washington right before his famous "I Have a Dream" speech. Says Rieder: "King recalled the lesson Prinz took from the Holocaust. 'When I was a rabbi of the Jewish community in Berlin under the Hitler regime...the most important thing that I learned in my life and under those tragic circumstances is that bigotry and hatred are not the most urgent problems. The most urgent, the most disgraceful, the most shameful, and the most tragic problem is silence.' A great people which created a great civilization had become a nation of silent onlookers who remained silent in the face of hate, in the face of brutality, and in the face of mass murder."[20]

My prayer is that the African American church will not remain silent as forces gather in the twenty-first century with the ultimate goal of destroying Israel. May it rise again with the same conviction, determination, and power that ushered in the power of new laws, new customs, and new rights that struck down long-standing racial discrimination and mistreatment. May we stand with our Jewish brothers in this hour in the same way that they marched alongside us during the 1950s and 1960s. May we speak out about the people God called "blessed" and vow that we will uphold their precious inheritance.

Chapter 5
VOID OF A VOICE:
MISLEADING THE AFRICAN
AMERICAN COMMUNITY

ONE OF THE tragedies in the African American community is the prevalence of anti-Semitism. How prevalent? Enough to draw a very public mention during a presidential election year. Less than ten months before voters selected him as president of the United States, Barack Obama told a crowd at historic Ebenezer Baptist Church in Atlanta that the black community needed—among other things—to do its part in fighting anti-Semitism, which he called a "scourge."

Speaking on the Martin Luther King holiday, the then senator said, "The scourge of anti-Semitism has, at times, revealed itself in our community. For too long, some of us have seen immigrants as competitors for jobs instead of companions in the fight for opportunity. Every day, our politics fuels and exploits this kind of division across all races and regions, across gender and party. It is played out on television. It is sensationalized by the media. And last week, it even crept into the campaign for President, with charges and counter-charges that served to obscure the issues instead of illuminating the critical choices we face as a nation."[1]

Various Jewish authors share such apprehensions. Writes well-known rabbi Sol Roth: "Anti-Semitism in the black community—among its members and leaders alike—has been increasing in recent years at an uncomfortable pace."[2] Author Elliott Abrams agrees that "anti-Semitism appears to be growing among American blacks, and although there has been little careful study of the problem, surveys suggest that 'black Americans remain considerably more likely than white Americans to hold anti-Semitic views.'"[3]

While it is true that too much of our nation's anti-Semitism originates in the African American community of which I am part, I also believe that too often the amplification of such voices make them the only ones America hears. Still these perceptions raise three crucial questions:

1. Why has the African American community not supported Israel in general?

2. Why has the African American church not supported Israel historically?

3. What fuels the anti-Semitism that is prominent in the African American community?

As I have already discussed, the Jewish and African American communities have a shared history of unique struggles and oppression. Jews have felt that they (more than any other group) could empathize with the plight of African Americans—and that African Americans would recognize this. Early in the twentieth century Jewish periodicals compared the African American movement for equality coming out of the South to the exodus of the Jews from Egypt. They noted that, like the Jews, African Americans:

- Lived in ghettos
- Faced dislocation from their ancient lands
- Suffered the same kind of victimization in the South that Jews did under various pogroms in Russia and Europe

So why the increase in anti-Semitism among African Americans, especially when it was the Jewish community that supported the African American community during some of its most challenging times? And especially when both communities have suffered horrendous persecution and unspeakable oppression? Our shared histories mean both groups should readily identify with the plights of dislocation, disenfranchisement, and disheartening circumstances. How disappointing when evidence arises that shows either side disregarding this reality.

There is also a spiritual dimension to our mutually shared identification. In the midst of such oppression and persecution, both communities embraced religion and spirituality in a search to find meaning in their lives. As noted earlier, historian Harold Brackman observes: "Though most Americans like to imagine our country as 'a promised land,' the Hebrew Bible's narratives of redemption from slavery and oppression have provided a special spiritual roadmap for two communities: African Americans and Jews who have struggled—often as allies—for civil rights and inclusion in the American Dream."[4]

Aligned With the Jewish Experience

From a spiritual perspective we can see how African Americans—since the early days of slavery—have aligned themselves with the Jewish experience. When we sing old spirituals like "Go Down, Moses" or "Wade in the Water," we draw parallels between our past plight in the South and that of the Jews in Egypt. Just as the children of Israel escaped from slavery and their taskmasters, so African Americans fought to escape slavery and the segregation that followed the Civil War. The popularity of the term *Zion* in many African American church names demonstrates our identification with the Jewish exodus from Egypt.

How sad, then, that too many African Americans ignore the lessons of history, some less than fifty years in the past. When people spit on us, when the police arrested us, when Bull Connor trained fire hoses on us and set loose his attack dogs in Birmingham, Jewish people boldly marched with us. They too faced all the hostility and venom segregationists could muster. As Johns Hopkins University scholar Joshua Muravchik writes, "The frontline troops in the Montgomery bus boycott and then in the lunch-counter sit-ins were all blacks, but among the whites who soon rallied to the cause, a large share—a disproportionate share—were Jews."[5]

According to Paul Berman, author of *Blacks and Jews*,

the Jewish community contributed one-half to three-fourths of the financial support given to civil rights groups and organizations.[6] As we learned earlier, Jews were key in the founding of the National Association for the Advancement of Colored People. And as reporter Christopher Reardon notes, Jews "figured more prominently than other whites in civil rights groups such as the Congress on Racial Equality and the Student Nonviolent Coordinating Committee."[7]

In the introduction I mentioned that nearly two-thirds of the non–African Americans who participated in the 1960s' Freedom Rides across the South were Jewish. About 50 percent of the civil rights attorneys in the South during the 1960s were Jewish. (Many of them—working at their own sacrificial expense—were jailed for standing for justice and civil rights.) More than 50 percent of the whites who went to Mississippi in 1964 to challenge voter intimidation and other Jim Crow laws were also Jewish.[8] Jews contributed financially toward many key African American organizations that stood for equality, which were crucial to the civil rights cause.

Those who might suggest that this support stemmed from idealism and self-interest fail to understand that Jews were largely committed to justice and fairness for all men. This justice, in turn, would improve their own plight. Says Rabbi Roth: "It is true that those people who engaged in the civil rights struggle derived personal satisfaction from their involvement, but that satisfaction hinged, by and large, not on the prospect of personal gain, but on the knowledge that they were conducting their lives in conformity with ethical principles to which they were committed."[9]

The Irony of Anti-Semitism

Ironically the same African Americans who espouse anti-Semitic views have suffered similar consequences stemming from distasteful prejudice, discrimination, and hateful rhetoric. There are several leading theories for the African American community's vulnerability to anti-Semitism. Among them are ignorance, perception, and socioeconomic envy. I believe too many African Americans fail to have a basic grasp of our shared history. Because they are not knowledgeable of Israel or the Jewish community's struggles with oppression, they are not inclined to stand with them.

Another possible motive for this lack of support is the views voiced by extremists who seem to routinely grab the spotlight as they proclaim the uniformed view that Jews have historically acted not as our ally but our enemy. Writes Roth: "The Jewish community today has two sources of strength available to it. One is economic, in the form of an impressive degree of prosperity; the other is political, in the form of a Jewish state. Distortion of the first leads to the view that the Jew is the slumlord; a distortion of the second yields the conclusion that the Jew is cruel. Both result in the judgment that the Jew is an oppressor."[10]

Roth says that in the black community, "because its hostility is rooted in economic and political factors, it is the most educated who are vulnerable to anti-Semitism.

They have the highest expectations and, therefore, the highest level of frustrations."[11] (I find it ironic and disturbing that better-educated sectors of our community demonstrate a lack of support for Israel and engage in anti-Semitic rhetoric, which runs contrary to findings by social science and community-relations experts.)

The probable motive of socioeconomic envy toward seemingly always-affluent Jews contributes to the lack of support for Israel. As Professor Muravchik notes: "Envy is a powerful emotion, and certainly when it comes to the Jews, blacks have much to be envious of. Measured by the standard of material or professional accomplishment, Jews are one of the most successful minorities in America, blacks one of the least.... To compound matters, though blacks have suffered far more prejudice and discrimination, Jews too have had to overcome barriers never faced by Gentile whites in America."[12] Such motivations may help explain why those of African descent worldwide— including those in the Caribbean Islands, South America, and Europe—warmly embrace the Jewish community, while many in the United States do not.

UCLA professor Eric Sundquist, author of multiple books on American culture, notes: "Even as Afro-Zionism modulated into black anti-Zionism at mid-century, some Black Power radicals remained divided in their identification between Jews and Arabs, Moses and Pharaoh."[13] While those of African descent worldwide have been led to embrace Israel and the Jewish community due to their biblical-theological understanding, many African Americans, unfortunately, have been led astray with the negative rhetoric and anti-Semitic propaganda of misinformed political and religious community leaders.

Reverends such as Jesse Jackson, Al Sharpton, and Jeremiah Wright have all earned reputations as anti-Semitic. During his presidential bid in 1984, Reverend Jackson referred to New York City as "Hymietown" in an interview with the *Washington Post*, remarks that stirred a storm of protest. Indeed, it caused such an uproar that a month later Jackson apologized to national Jewish leaders gathered at a synagogue in Manchester, New Hampshire.[14]

Years later investigative reporter and best-selling author Kenneth Timmerman labeled Jackson as "a danger to American Jews, the state of Israel, and to America itself."[15] Recalling Jackson's presidential bid, Timmerman wrote, "Jackson blamed media criticism of his finances on the Jews. Saying that he wanted to 'talk black talk,' Jackson confided in black reporter Milton Coleman that he was being unfairly treated by the 'Hymies' who controlled the media. The worst of all was the *New York Times*, but what could you expect from 'Hymietown'?"[16]

Another self-proclaimed preacher, Sharpton has taken anti-Semitic stances, going back more than two decades. He was heatedly criticized as an agitator after the unfortunate accidental death in August of 1991 of a seven-year-old black American boy. Gavin Cato was struck and killed by a car in the motorcade of Menachem Mendel Scheerson, a prominent Hasidic rabbi and leader in an Orthodox Jewish movement known as Chabad-Lubavitch. In the three-day-long Crown Heights riots that followed, several Jews were seriously injured, and Yankel Rosenbaum,

a Jewish history scholar visiting from Australia, was
stabbed to death. Another man mistakenly identified as
an Orthodox Jew was murdered two weeks later, in the
aftermath of the riots.[17]

Fanning Discontent

In an article about a panel discussion reflecting on black-
Jewish relations two decades later, the *Jewish Journal* mentioned the accusations leveled against Sharpton—that
he helped fuel three days of riots with his actions and
remarks after the accident. The report noted, "He led a
protest march of hundreds shouting 'no justice, no peace'
through the streets of Crown Heights to the Lubavitcher
movement's world headquarters. After the riots had sub-
sided, at [Gavin] Cato's funeral, he referred to the neigh-
borhood's Chasidic Jews as 'diamond merchants.'"[18]

The article quoted Norman Rosenbaum (Yankel Rosenbaum's brother) as saying, "[Sharpton] did absolutely
nothing then to improve black-Jewish relations—and
nothing since."[19] That same week Sharpton admitted that
he made "mistakes" during the Crown Heights riots, commenting, "Twenty years later, I have grown. I would still
have stood up for Gavin Cato, but I would have included
in my utterances that there was no justification or excuse
for violence or the death of Yankel Rosenbaum."[20]

It is my sincerest hope and prayer today that Reverend
Sharpton finally now understands and appreciates the
unique parallels between the two communities. Reverend
Sharpton should continually and boldly stand against

injustice at all times. However, may his stance include supporting the Jewish community.

Anti-Semitism and anti-Israel sentiments have also emerged from Jeremiah Wright, President Obama's former pastor who made insensitive remarks about the Jewish community after the 2008 presidential campaign. In a June 2009 interview with the *Daily Press* of Hampton Roads, Virginia, Wright said that he "did not expect to have any contact with his former congregant, President Barack Obama, until he was a lame duck or out of office because 'them Jews ain't going to let him talk to me.' He went on to blame the American Israel Public Affairs Council (AIPAC) for the estrangement between himself and Obama." Wright didn't stop there, adding, "Ethnic cleansing is going on in Gaza. Ethnic cleansing [by] the Zionist is a sin and a crime against humanity, and they don't want Barack talking like that because that's anti-Israel."[21]

Though not a Christian leader, in recent times Muslim Minister Louis Farrakhan has served as the most outspoken critic of the Jewish people. The face of black anti-Semitism, the Nation of Islam leader in 1984 labeled Hitler a "great man." Michael Kotzin, executive vice president of the Jewish United Fund and Jewish Federation of Metropolitan Chicago, comments: "Farrakhan and his followers are giving new life to traditional anti-Semitic notions of Jewish conspiracies, of Jewish control and of Jewish villainy. This form of anti-Semitism comes not from experience or fact but from certain earlier images about Jews which have taken on mythic potency and which fit Farra-khan's worldview."[22]

Adds *Faith or Fear* author Elliott Abrams: "Leaders such as Louis Farrakhan voice the most vicious anti-Semitic sentiments, and these words have not rendered Farrakhan and his colleagues untouchables for the black political establishment. This anti-Semitic message has received a sympathetic hearing from all too many black audiences—not least on college campuses, where tomorrow's black elites are being educated."[23]

Farrakhan's leadership has inspired individuals like Khalid Abdul Muhammad, a spokesman for the Nation of Islam who has fueled continued animosity and hatred toward the Jewish community. Kotzin of the Jewish United Fund believes Muhammad is reinforcing the views of Farrakhan with statements such as "the so-called Jew...is sucking our blood in the black community."[24] Scholar Joshua Muravchik offers this lament: "From Jesse Jackson's 'Hymietown' remarks, to...Louis Farrakhan, the anti-Semitic virus has crept closer and closer to the center of black consciousness."[25]

While I cannot deny the existence of such sentiments in the African American community, I am saddened by the fact that the aforementioned leaders have generally been the only voices representing black America on the national scene. Since there has been too little vocal support for Israel from the African American community—especially from our pulpits—too many observers are easily left with the impression that such expressions represent most African Americans. One of my leading goals is to gather others who will stand up and express an opposing view.

Empathy for Palestine

Regardless of whether they feel apathetic about Israel or resist the biblical record identifying the Jews as inheritors of God's covenant, many African Americans today seem to particularly empathize with Palestinians. They see them as victims, comparable to those in our community who struggled during the civil rights era. As I stated in my dedication, I am aware and sensitive to the plight of Palestinians, especially those Christians who feel trapped in the crossfire of conflict. That is why I like to remind others that it is not Israel that oppresses the Palestinians. It is the leaders of Palestine who oppress their own people through their adamant refusal to consider compromise with Israel, which stands ready and willing to achieve peace in the Middle East.

Numerous ethnicities and cultures make up the general population of the Middle East. In the case of Palestine, that includes Arabs and Jews. Still, too many African Americans fail to grasp the biblical and historical significance of the conflict between Muslims and Jews that is behind this continuing struggle. As Christians our community should be courageous enough to address the biblical references concerning the historical relationship between the Judeo-Christian and Muslim faiths, since this will shed light on the continuing friction.

Many biblical scholars trace the origin of the Muslim people back to Ishmael, the son of Abraham and his wife's maid Hagar (Gen. 16:11). Islamists also believe that Ishmael is the traditional ancestor of Muhammad and the Arab people. In Genesis Moses described Ishmael as a "wild donkey of a man" whose hand would be against everyone and everyone's hand against him, a man who would live in hostility toward all his brothers (v. 12). Moses also recorded that Abram cast out both Hagar and her child, Ishmael. Many scholars suggest because of the later birth of Isaac (Gen. 21), the covenant God established with Abraham would continue through Isaac and not Ishmael:

> The child grew and was weaned, and on the day Isaac was weaned Abraham held a great feast. But Sarah saw that the son whom Hagar the Egyptian had borne to Abraham was mocking, and she said to Abraham, "Get rid of that slave woman and her son, for that slave woman's son will never share in the inheritance with my son Isaac." The matter distressed Abraham greatly because it concerned his son. But God said to him, "Do not be so distressed about the boy and your maidservant. Listen to whatever Sarah tells you, because it is through Isaac that your offspring will be reckoned."
>
> —GENESIS 21:8–12

This direct line of covenant with Israel also appears in the narrative of Jacob and Esau. Once again God makes a clear distinction that—like Ishmael—Esau was destined to live outside of God's covenant with Israel. When Esau asked him about the blessings that accompany

God's promises, Isaac delivered a historic response (which prompted his older son to deliver a vow of revenge):

> His father Isaac answered him, "Your dwelling will be away from the earth's richness, away from the dew of heaven above. You will live by the sword and you will serve your brother. But when you grow restless, you will throw his yoke from off your neck." Esau held a grudge against Jacob because of the blessing his father had given him. He said to himself, "The days of mourning for my father are near; then I will kill my brother Jacob."
>
> —GENESIS 27:39–41

As it does with Ishmael, the Bible spells out how Esau is considered an "outside" son, rejected from the lineage of blessings and covenant. Both Ishmael and Esau contemplated threats toward their brothers, Isaac and Jacob. Ironically Ishmael was the older son preferred by his father, Abraham, just as Esau was the older son preferred by his father, Isaac. Yet Isaac and then Jacob were honored and preferred by their respective mothers, Sarah and Rebekah.

Nine chapters after Esau made his vow, we read about the birth of his grandson Amalek, born to Esau's son Eliphaz and his concubine (Gen. 36:12). Amalek and his descendants, the Amalekites, proved to be a continuing adversary to the nation of Israel, as outlined in Deuteronomy, when God spoke to Moses:

> Remember what the Amalekites did to you along the way when you came out of Egypt. When you

were weary and worn out, they met you on your
journey and cut off all who were lagging behind;
they had no fear of God. When the LORD your
God gives you rest from all the enemies around
you in the land he is giving you to possess as an
inheritance, you shall blot out the memory of
Amalek from under heaven. Do not forget!

—DEUTERONOMY 25:17–19

Amalek and the Amalekites serve as a prototype for all
anti-Semites. Agag was king of the Amalekites, a tribal
people living in the Negev and the Sinai Peninsula. The
Amalekites had attacked the Israelites in the wilderness
and were therefore cursed (according to Exodus 17:14).
In Numbers 24:7 "Agag" refers to the Amalekite people.
Agag was a common name among Amalekite kings. Many
Bible scholars suggest that Haman, an archenemy of
Israel, was a descendant of the Amalekites. They cite the
story outlined in the Book of Esther, which calls Haman
an Agagite (Esther 3:1), a descendant of Agag. Given this
lineage, it is no surprise that Haman tried to destroy the
Jews before Esther exposed his diabolical plot and he
wound up swinging from the gallows he hoped would cru-
cify the Jewish leader Mordecai.

This important fact is also reestablished in the New
Testament as Paul reconfirms and reinforces God's unique
and unilateral covenant with Abram in Galatians 4:21–31:

Tell me, you who want to be under the law, are you
not aware of what the law says? For it is written
that Abraham had two sons, one by the slave

woman and the other by the free woman. His son by the slave woman was born in the ordinary way; but his son by the free woman was born as the result of a promise.

These things may be taken figuratively, for the women represent two covenants. One covenant is from Mount Sinai and bears children who are to be slaves: This is Hagar. Now Hagar stands for Mount Sinai in Arabia and corresponds to the present city of Jerusalem, because she is in slavery with her children. But the Jerusalem that is above is free, and she is our mother. For it is written: "Be glad, O barren woman, who bears no children; break forth and cry aloud, you who have no labor pains; because more are the children of the desolate woman than of her who has a husband."

Now you, brothers, like Isaac, are children of promise. At that time the son born in the ordinary way persecuted the son born by the power of the Spirit. It is the same now. But what does the Scripture say? "Get rid of the slave woman and her son, for the slave woman's son will never share in the inheritance with the free woman's son." Therefore, brothers, we are not children of the slave woman, but of the free woman.

As partial and inequitable as it may seem, God has clearly established for the Christian and Jewish believers the promises of blessings, inheritance, and freedom through the line of Abraham, Isaac, and Jacob.

Courting Arabs

One might ask: If the black and Jewish communities have so much in common, why do so many African Americans seem to side with Arab Palestinians? How did this favoritism come to exist? I believe much of this empathy originated in the late 1950s through the influence of the popular African American leader Elijah Muhammad and the Nation of Islam. Favorable toward Egyptian President Gamal Abdel Nasser as a long-lost Muslim brother and identifying with a face of color, Muhammad praised Nasser for standing up against British and French imperialism. Flying in the face of historical fact, Muhammad taught that Jesus was not a Jew (though he meant Jesus was not a white Jew, because he believed only black Jews were born in Palestine).

Historian Harold Blackman writes of Muhammad's visit to Egypt: "Officially invited by Nasser, Elijah Muhammad met with the Egyptian President in late 1959, convincing him that the [Nation of Islam] was an ideal instrument for propagating the Arab cause against Israel in the U.S."[26] Later Malcolm X—then a top minister in the Nation of Islam—would make his own pilgrimage to Mecca and Egypt. While there Malcolm X, whose rise to fame ultimately resulted in his assassination by Nation of Islam members, encouraged Arabs to reach out to the African American community in the United States. He hoped that in return, blacks would empathize with the Arab cause.

Such pilgrimages fueled growing anti-Jewish sentiment

in African American communities in the 1960s and 1970s, helped along by the Pan-African and Black Nationalist movements. The extreme criticism of Israel derived from these movements sparked an eclectic mixture among many blacks of apathy and animosity toward Jews.

Despite these currents of hostility, such prominent leaders as Martin Luther King Jr. continued to embrace Israel. In an interview with *Conservative Judaism* in 1968, King remarked, "I see Israel, and never mind saying it, as one of the great outposts of democracy in the world, and a marvelous example of what can be done, how desert land can almost be transformed into an oasis of brotherhood and democracy. Peace for Israel means security and that security must be a reality."[27]

Such comments illustrate one of the little-publicized yet quietly tragic elements of Dr. King's untimely death in the spring of 1968. Namely, that his assassination extinguished a leading light of support for Israel in our community. Thanks to the anti-Semitic perspectives voiced by noted African American leaders, the 1970s saw the dimming of support for the Jewish people. Perhaps it is no coincidence that when Dr. King died we saw a growing empathy for Palestinians. Reverend Jackson's 1979 Middle Eastern peace overture via a trip to Lebanon, Libya, and other Arab nations was but one effort that helped advance this sentiment. While supposedly aimed at brokering peace and harmony, the trip largely became a photo op for Jackson, who was famously photographed embracing Arafat.

Jackson would go on to muddy the waters of diplomacy

by seeking out funds from Arab-American supporters for his PUSH organization after the fall of the shah of Iran in 1979. Just before his departure from the Middle East, Jackson warned the PLO leaders that the support of the African American community was essential: "By October 1, there will be no black leader left willing to come to the aid of the Palestinian cause, if there is not an immediate infusion of funds into the black community from Arab states...we will all learn to recite the alphabet without three letters, P-L-O."[28] Jackson's tactics worked: several gifts, large and small, materialized for PUSH from Arab supporters.

What Really Happened

Unfortunately little of this money ever made its way into the African American community. Although African Americans witnessing these developments warmed to the idea of relating to the Arab world, Bishop Lemuel Thuston—a historian in the Church of God in Christ— says, "It is overwhelmingly obvious that little to no financial aid, nor funds were given to the African American people during the civil rights days from the Palestinians...while it was the Jewish people that stood up for blacks and gave liberally to their causes and organizations. Yet we as blacks want to side with the Palestinian struggle.[29]

Thuston's recent remarks confirm an earlier finding by the Pew Center for the People and the Press. In a study of Christian clergy from nineteen major denominations (including several leading African American groups), the center posed several questions regarding support for Israel and views on Middle East policy. Political science professor James Guth said the findings of African American Protestant clergy "present a more complex picture." As a group, these pastors are narrowly split with less than a third favoring Israel, less than a third favoring the Palestinians, and a little more than a third "not sure."[30]

In my own travels across the United States over the last several years I have observed much the same trend. However, I have found that more African American clergy tend to favor Israel than the Palestinians. It is also quite obvious that many ministers simply don't know what to think or believe.

Leading Zionists such as attorney and political commentator Alan Dershowitz, Israeli professor and historian Benny Morris, and Israel's former United Nations ambassador Dore Gold agree on the complexities of the Palestinian problems facing Israel:

- Dershowitz, who considers himself both pro-Israel and pro-Palestinian, writes, "Today Israel is seen by many European Jews as a source of danger, because anti-Zionism has become the current justification or excuse for violence against Jews. This has resulted in some fair-weather supporters of Israel abandoning their support during difficult times."[31]

- Says Morris: "A country divided between Israelis on the one hand and on the other

Palestinians who had returned and were filled with anger not only at the way they had been treated in the past but also at not finding their villages or homes available— that country would quickly become ungovernable. Each individual Jew living in the country would be facing a real physical danger."[32]

♦ Gold, now president of the Jerusalem Center for Public Affairs, believes that many in the Palestinian community have the detriment of Israel in mind with their plans to seek unilateral statehood with the support of the United Nations. He writes, "The real importance of any new UN General Assembly resolution is the follow-up the Palestinians pursue...that Israeli settlements and military bases in the West Bank will no longer be 'occupiers' but rather 'invaders' in a sovereign state. Might Israel be subject to sanctions?"[33]

It has been both alarming and unnerving to me, as an African American pastor, to see the comparisons made between the Palestinian movement in Israel and the civil rights struggle of the 1950s and 1960s. Unfortunately many people want to believe that Israel is oppressing and systematically persecuting the Arab Palestinian people. They hope to sway unaware and uninformed people, many who have never traveled to the Middle East, to buy into the propaganda that Israel is unfair and unjust toward Arab Palestinians.

In April 2012 media reports circulated that Israel was responsible for persecuting Palestinian Christians in Bethlehem and beyond. Yet I have talked with Israelis on the ground who say it is the Palestinian Authority that is failing to defend the interests of Christians. As Christians flee persecution in Iraq, Jordan, Syria, and elsewhere in the Middle East, they are running into Israel because they have more freedom there than in any of the other surrounding nations, which are dominated by Muslim leadership.

As I have adamantly said, it is not the Israelis who are persecuting or oppressing the Palestinians; it's the Palestinian leaders who oppress the Palestinian people. And instead of reporting the fact, the media in the West are painting a distorted picture. It would be a tragedy for Christians to buy into the lies and media hype, and see Israel perish as a result.

Chapter 6

ISRAEL'S ENEMIES
THROUGH THE AGES

D ID IRAN PRESIDENT Mahmoud Ahmadinejad once
declare that Israel should be wiped off the face of the
map? Although widely reported since 2005, a more recent
story in the *Washington Post* says such claims—which
originated with a story in the *New York Times*—stemmed
from a misinterpretation of Ahmadinejad's remarks. The
Post cited statements by University of Michigan history
professor Juan Cole and Arash Norouzi, cofounder of
the Mossadegh Project. They contend that Ahmadinejad's original statement in Persian did not say that Israel
should be wiped off the face of the map, but that it would
collapse.

In a lengthy article on the Mossadegh Project's website, Norouzi objected to reporting of the remark (which,
ironically, came from Iran's propaganda arm, the Islamic
Republic News Agency). He writes that Ahmadinejad
never referred to Israel the country or Israel the land-
mass, but the Israeli regime. Norouzi notes that the quotation in question was itself a quote from the late Ayatollah
Ruhollah Khomeini, the father of the Islamic Revolution.
Thus, he says, Ahmadinejad was credited with a quote that

represents a viewpoint well in place well before he ever took office.

"Ahmadinejad does not even refer to Israel by name, he instead uses the specific phrase 'rezhim-e ishghalgar-e qods' (regime occupying Jerusalem)," Norouzi says. "So this raises the question...what exactly did he want 'wiped from the map'? The answer is: *nothing.* That's because the word 'map' was *never used.* The Persian word for map, '*nagsheh*', is not contained anywhere in his original Farsi quote, or, for that matter, anywhere in his entire speech. Nor was the western phrase 'wipe out' ever said. Yet we are led to believe that Iran's President threatened to 'wipe Israel off the map', despite never having uttered the words 'map', 'wipe out' or even 'Israel'."[1]

To paraphrase a well-known quotation from Shakespeare's *Hamlet*, methinks Norouzi doth protest too much. The *Post* story chronicled how, following the widely reported remark, Iranian government entities erected billboards and signs with the "wipe off" phrase in English. An official with the Jerusalem Center for Public Affairs even compiled a collection of photographs of these banners, including one on the building housing military reserves of the Islamic Revolutionary Guard Corps reading, "Israel should be wiped out of the face of the world." Glenn Kessler, author of "The Fact Checker" column for the *Washington Post*, recalled that in 2000 Iranian Supreme Leader Ayatollah Ali Khamenei said that Iran's position is that Israel must be uprooted from the region.

"Clearly, the Iranian government has unrelenting opposition to the state of Israel, so much so that it even rejects

Palestinian efforts at statehood if that would result in Israel remaining in the Middle East," Kessler wrote. "Indeed, Tehran has armed and funded Hamas, Hezbollah and other militant groups opposed to Israel. At the same time, the words allegedly uttered by Ahmadinejad have been used to suggest a change toward a more militaristic posture by Iran toward Israel....Khamenei, in fact, has been consistent in speaking of his hatred of Israel, but without a military context."[2]

A Dangerous Situation

As far as I'm concerned, arguing over the exact translation of Ahmadinejad's remarks when he assumed the presidency of Iran is parsing words while overlooking the big picture. To pretend that Iran and fellow Islamists in the Middle East aren't dedicated to the ultimate destruction of Israel is to ignore reality. It is to turn a blind eye to the continuing threats against Israel, as demonstrated by Egyptian President Mohammed Morsi recently participating in prayers urging Allah to destroy the Jews and their supporters.[3] Such comments illustrate how the situation evolving on the worldwide stage threatens Israel and the United States. Yet far too many of our leaders ignore the vile threats posed by radical jihadists. The slumbering apathy of diplomacy-driven Western leaders and a lethargic attitude by US political and spiritual leaders could make for a disastrous combination.

A startling example of the ends to which these extremists will go appeared not too long ago. In a *World* magazine article titled "Stealth Jihadists," journalist Warren

Cole Smith traced the development of an insidious brand of socially responsible investing called Sharia-compliant finance (SCF). In the Christian vernacular, "socially responsible investing" refers to funds that avoid objectionable stocks, such as those of companies involved in abortion, tobacco, alcohol, or pornography. There are funds for every imaginable taste. Investors can avoid companies they find distasteful (i.e., weapons and military projects) or support those in line with their values, such as "green" funds backing environmentally sustainable operations.

However, Sharia-compliant finance comes with a unique twist. One requirement of Sharia law is to fund jihad. "So these funds are helping to kill American soldiers," observes Kevin Freeman, who formerly worked for the late Sir John Templeton (a noted investor who avoided tobacco and other "sin" stocks).[4]

Nor is SCF a brand-new development. Smith's article reveals that in 2000 stock market giant Dow Jones created the Dow Jones Islamic Fund, a Sharia-compliant mutual fund. Retail brokerage firms Charles Schwab, TD Waterhouse, and AmeriTrade offer the fund to their customers. This brings a warning from Rachel Ehrenfeld of the American Center for Democracy's Economic Warfare Institute that such concentrated wealth has the power to disrupt global markets, particularly because of these funds' notable lack of transparency. "She believes Sharia funds could be the source of the so-called 'flash crashes' that occasionally afflict the markets," Smith writes. "A joint report by the Securities and Exchange Commission Futures Trading Commission could not rule out terrorism as a cause for a May 6, 2010, crash that caused the Dow to drop 1,000 points."[5]

Aside from the mind-boggling nature of Western nations turning a blind eye to such work, Sharia-compliant funds demonstrate the dogged determination of militant Islamists. No matter what their innocuous-sounding public statements, they are seeking to fulfill their Allah-given assignment to rid the world of "infidels" and "illegitimates." Commenting on the existential threat Iran poses for both Israel and the United States, Princeton University Professor Bernard Lewis says, "There is a sort of a cultural relativism in the West that makes people reluctant to condemn, particular to condemn another civilization, we must be nice to them, we must be tolerant, we must be understanding and so forth...but this should not go to the level of blinding ourselves to the more painful realities of the situation."[6]

As a nation where millions come from a historic Judeo-Christian background, many in the United States don't grasp the idea of jihad-driven agenda or holy war in the name of a supreme ruler or deity. Clifford May, a journalist and president of the Foundation for Defense of Democracies, says, "Americans and Europeans are really uncomfortable with the idea of holy wars and mass murders for religious reasons.... They can't imagine themselves slaughtering other human beings because the true religion needs to defeat the enemies of God. Because they can't imagine that for themselves, they also can't imagine that others behave that way...but this is the failure of imagination."[7]

Today when one listens to the seemingly harmless, innocent rhetoric of radical Islamic groups, too many Americans tend to give that person or group the benefit of the doubt. Given jihadists' clear intent, such a stance is foolish. No longer can we ignore the deeper implications of statements like this one from Iranian Ayatollah Ali Khamenei: "The Islamic Republic's proposal to help resolve the Palestinian issue and heal this old wound is a clear and logical initiative based on political concepts accepted by world public opinion, which has already been presented in detail. We do not suggest launching a classic war by the armies of Muslim countries, or throwing immigrant Jews into the sea, or mediation by the UN and other international organizations. We propose holding a referendum with [the participation of] the Palestinian nation. The Palestinian nation, like any other nation, has the right to determine their own destiny and elect the governing system of the country."[8]

The call for free and fair elections may sound peaceful and democratic. Unfortunately looking on the surface and failing to discern the intentions of the speaker represents an ill-advised and historically uninformed perspective. When it comes to terrorists and evil dictators, trying to placate or negotiate with them is a recipe for disaster. We need only to hearken back to 1938 and the Munich Agreement, when France and England failed to stand up to Adolf Hitler and agreed to Germany's annexing Czechoslovakia's Sudetenland region. Hitler then invaded Poland, which sparked the onset of World War II.

Anti-Semitic Rulers

Historically and consistently, when evil dictators say they want to kill, annihilate, or destroy a people, usually they say what they mean and mean what they say. Such was the case for two destructive dictators of the past who were bent on destroying the Jews.

Some twenty-five hundred years ago, Haman—the prime minister of Persia (which is modern-day Iran)—was the evil ruler plotting to destroy the Jews. The Book of Esther describes how this heroine joined forces with her cousin, Mordecai, to defeat Haman and his murderous plans. Ironically the very gallows that Haman designed in hopes of hanging Mordecai wound up becoming the instrument of Haman's death. Though the name "God" is neither mentioned nor referenced in Esther, one can clearly see the providential hand of God in thematic form, especially on the life of beautiful, courageous Esther and her perceptive cousin:

> When Esther's words were reported to Mordecai, he sent back this answer: "Do not think that because you are in the king's house you alone of all the Jews will escape. For if you remain silent at this time, relief and deliverance for the Jews will arise from another place, but you and your father's family will perish. And who knows but that you have come to royal position for such a time as this?"
>
> Then Esther sent this reply to Mordecai: "Go, gather together all the Jews who are in Susa, and fast for me. Do not eat or drink for three days, night or day. I and my maids will fast as you do. When this is done, I will go to the king, even though it is against the law. And if I perish, I perish."
>
> —ESTHER 4:12–16

Those who have read the story know the outcome. Esther's courage in the face of possible death, coupled with Mordecai's strategic wisdom, ultimately caused the Jews to defeat the plot by their enemy. Although the king wouldn't reverse the death order that Haman cunningly convinced him to issue, he gave a second command allowing the Jews to defend themselves:

> On the thirteenth day of the twelfth month, the month of Adar, the edict commanded by the king was to be carried out. On this day the enemies of the Jews had hoped to overpower them, but now the tables were turned and the Jews got the upper hand over those who hated them. The Jews assembled in their cities in all the provinces of King Xerxes to attack those seeking their destruction. No one could stand against them, because the people of all the other nationalities were afraid of them. And all the nobles of the provinces, the satraps, the governors and the king's administrators helped the Jews, because fear of Mordecai had seized them. Mordecai was prominent in the palace; his reputation spread throughout the provinces, and he became more and more powerful.
>
> The Jews struck down all their enemies with the sword, killing and destroying them, and they did what they pleased to those who hated them.
>
> —ESTHER 9:1–5

Haman proved the ancient forerunner of Hitler, just as Hitler symbolized the diabolical spirit that drove Haman by continuing his pattern of hatred and cruel plotting against the Jews. Like Haman thousands of years before him, Hitler desired a superrace of Aryan people and sought to eliminate the Jewish population. And, like Haman, Hitler ended up dying in disgrace, though the details of his suicide remain unclear. The demise of these two leaders is evidence of a divine hand working to reverse plots against His children. God continually demonstrates how the enemies of Israel will ultimately wind up tilting against windmills.

Though *Washington Post* columnist Kessler suggests Ayatollah Khamenei is the power broker in Iran, President Ahmadinejad still wears the public face as the modern-day symbol of Haman and Hitler. Those who quibble over whether Iran's president said Israel should be wiped off the face of the earth should pay attention to the full context of his remarks, made before an audience of four thousand students at a program titled "The World Without Zionism." The 2005 *New York Times* article reported that Ahmadinejad's tone was reminiscent of the early days of Iran's Islamic Revolution in 1979, after which anti-Israel slogans became common at rallies.

"Senior officials had avoided provocative language over the past decade, but Ahmadinejad appears to be taking a more confrontational tone than Iranian leaders have in recent years," the *Times* wrote. "Ahmadinejad said in his remarks Wednesday that the issue of a Palestinian state would be resolved only when Palestinians took control of all their lands. 'The establishment of Zionist regime was a move by the world oppressor against the Islamic world,' he said, according to the [Iranian] press agency.

"The skirmishes in the occupied land are part of the war of destiny. The outcome of hundreds of years of war will be defined in Palestinian land.'" Later in the speech he added, "Anybody who recognizes Israel will burn in the fire of the Islamic nation's fury." Any Islamic leader "who recognizes the Zionist regime means he is acknowledging the surrender and defeat of the Islamic world."9

Such hateful rhetoric shows how the same cry rings forth in the twenty-first century as it did in the days of Esther and Mordecai. We need the same kind of people of influence who will rise up and realize their destined place: to be positioned for God's kingdom and stand up for the Jews—for such a time as this.

Grave Similarities

It is not difficult to observe the grave similarities among Haman, Hitler, and Ahmadinejad. These three rulers share a lineage of opposition and adversaries one can trace back through the Old Testament, long before Haman's era. As I mentioned in the previous chapter, over the years Amalek has served as the prototype for anti-Semites. However, the passage I quoted from Deuteronomy 25:17–19 wasn't the only time that God instructed Israel to strike the Amalekites. The prophet Samuel delivered a similar message to Saul, Israel's first king.

> Samuel said to Saul, "I am the one the LORD sent to anoint you king over his people Israel; so listen now to the message from the LORD. This is what the LORD Almighty says: 'I will punish the

Amalekites for what they did to Israel when they
waylaid them as they came up from Egypt. Now go,
attack the Amalekites and totally destroy everything that belongs to them. Do not spare them;
put to death men and women, children and infants,
cattle and sheep, camels and donkeys.'"

—1 Samuel 15:1–3

Some biblical critics find fault with a God who would
direct Israel to completely wipe out an enemy. By doing so
they miss the point: Saul disobeyed a direct order from
the One who chose him to reign over His chosen people.
Nor was it simply defiance; greed also drove Saul to avoid
compliance. This is the kind of action that retains rele-
vance in the twenty-first century. Refusing to follow God's
directions can result in sad consequences years later, just
as it did in Saul's case.

Then Saul attacked the Amalekites all the way
from Havilah to Shur, to the east of Egypt. He
took Agag king of the Amalekites alive, and all
his people he totally destroyed with the sword.
But Saul and the army spared Agag and the best
of the sheep and cattle, the fat calves and lambs—
everything that was good. These they were
unwilling to destroy completely, but everything
that was despised and weak they totally destroyed.

—1 Samuel 15:7–9

Since the Lord had ordered the complete destruction
of the Amalekites, Samuel later rebuked Saul for his disobedience and reported God's rejection of Saul as king of

Israel. Then Samuel took up a sword and executed Agag. The consequences of Saul failing to carry out the divine order surface later when these same Amalekites attack David and his men.

> David and his men reached Ziklag on the third day. Now the Amalekites had raided the Negev and Ziklag. They had attacked Ziklag and burned it, and had taken captive the women and all who were in it, both young and old. They killed none of them, but carried them off as they went on their way. When David and his men came to Ziklag, they found it destroyed by fire and their wives and sons and daughters taken captive. So David and his men wept aloud until they had no strength left to weep.
>
> —I Samuel 30:1–4

Of course, King David is no Saul, so he seeks wise counsel from the priest Abiathar. Then David pursued his enemies and recovered everything they stole.

> David fought them from dusk until the evening of the next day, and none of them got away, except four hundred young men who rode off on camels and fled. David recovered everything the Amalekites had taken, including his two wives. Nothing was missing: young or old, boy or girl, plunder or anything else they had taken. David brought everything back.
>
> —I Samuel 30:17–19

The Remnant

Despite his best attempt, David didn't destroy *all* of his enemies, with four hundred young men escaping on camels. The Amalekites reappeared continually throughout Scripture, including in the Book of Esther. As referenced previously, many scholars suggest that in the Book of Esther Haman is described as a physical descendent of Amalek. Through his descendants the spirit of Haman has afflicted Israel over the last several thousand years.

God's warning long ago to destroy the Amalekites has even greater implications today. Instead of men armed with rocks and slings, modern dictators and terrorists are plotting and scheming to acquire nuclear weaponry. Could it possibly be that history is repeating itself, with a lack of preventative actions to destroy the enemies of freedom and democracy manifesting itself in potentially cataclysmic consequences? With such inaction we have modern-day Iran, which represents an existential threat to Israel. We also have Hamas and Hezbollah, enemies of Israel with clearly stated objectives urging her demise.

Nor is this a recent development. In 1928 the Muslim Brotherhood birthed the creed, "Allah is our objective. The Prophet is our leader. Koran is our law. Jihad is our way. Dying in the way of Allah is our highest hope."[10] According to a report quoting Mosab Hassan Yousef, the son of a Hamas cofounder: "Forget about what the Muslim Brotherhood, what al-Qaida, what Hezbollah—what even Americans or Westerners say about Islam. Let's study and see what Islam says about itself, then we will understand why we have this problem.... [The Muslim Brotherhood] will keep the hope and the ultimate goal very clear in the eyes of every Muslim who belongs to the organization that one day [we will] establish an Islamic state and establish Sharia law.... If they can establish this in a peaceful manner, that's fine.... But they are required by the Quran to establish this global Islamic state on the rubble of every civilization, every constitution, every government."[11]

Where does this leave Israel and allies like the United States? Living in a dangerous situation. No matter how much people may pretend otherwise, the advocates of freedom and democracy face the threat of violence and dictatorship from Islamist radicals and terrorists with a jihadist agenda. Any threat or attack against Israel, the "little Satan," is an attack against the United States of America, the "big Satan." While we as Christians cannot afford to yield to fear and intimidation, neither can we remain silent. Will we, as Dr. Martin Luther King Jr. once said, "have to repent in this generation not merely for the hateful words and actions of the bad people, but for the appalling silence of the good people"?[12]

If we in the West do not awaken and courageously speak up on behalf of Israel, the same apathy and non-activism that have existed in the past will again prove to be disadvantageous and detrimental. Dr. King rightly noted that "peace for Israel means security, and we must stand with all our might to protect her right to exist, its territorial integrity and the right to use whatever sea lanes it needs.... Peace for Israel means security, and that security must be a reality."[13]

Chapter 7

THE ISRAEL APARTHEID QUESTION

THE ANTI-SEMITIC, ANTI-ISRAEL sentiment gathering steam in the United States and elsewhere demonstrates a carefully orchestrated campaign to dehumanize, delegitimize, and demonize Israel. One of the leading claims voiced for years by Israel's critics is that the Jewish nation has enforced the evils of the same apartheid that once reined in South Africa. Rather than seeing as legitimate their comparison of Israel to the vile South African system that caused so much suffering for forty-six years, I consider the critics guilty of oversimplification.

Playing the "apartheid card" is a carefully designed attempt to conjure up images associated with the racist South African regime of the twentieth century. To quickly rebut such claims, let me define apartheid. It is an oppressive legal system of separation based on race and ethnicity, or institutionalized segregation and discrimination. It also involves inhuman acts committed for the purpose of establishing and maintaining domination by one racial group over another for the purpose of systematically oppressing them.

Under apartheid in South Africa black South Africans

could not vote and had few legal rights, even though they represented the majority of the country's population. Unlike blacks in apartheid South Africa, Arabs in Israel can go anywhere they want. They can use public transportation, eat in restaurants, go to swimming pools, use libraries, and go to cinemas alongside Jews—something no blacks could do in South Africa.

Still, these claims persist, spreading their tentacles around the world's consciousness. They are fueled by figures such as South African Archbishop Desmond Tutu. Winner of the Nobel Peace Prize in 1984 amid his outspoken criticism of apartheid, the internationally known cleric also won the Presidential Medal of Freedom in 2009. After visiting the Holy Land in 2002, he told an audience in Boston that he had witnessed the humiliation of Palestinians at checkpoints and roadblocks. He compared that to the suffering he and other South Africans endured during apartheid.

Noting that Jews had been at the forefront of the struggle against apartheid, Tutu asked, "Have our Jewish sisters and brothers forgotten their humiliation? Have they forgotten the collective punishment, the home demolitions, in their own history so soon? Have they turned their backs on their profound and noble religious traditions?"[1]

Bishop Tutu has maintained this stance throughout the years, supporting such moves as a widespread campaign to convince American pension funds and other parties to divest their holdings in companies doing business in Israel. Though rooted in fallacy, this pressure has mounted and in many cases succeeded. When pension giant TIAA-CREF held its 2011 national meeting in Charlotte, North Carolina (a year before the Democratic National Convention convened there), protesters amassed outside the event.

In an op-ed published by the *Charlotte Observer* just prior to the meeting, Tutu wrote, "The campaign originated with a call from the American group Jewish Voice for Peace, whose members understand that ending the occupation means a better future for both Israelis and Palestinians; a future in which both the violence of the occupier and the violent resistance of the occupied come to an end, where one people no longer rule over another, and where the cycles of suffering, humiliation and retaliation are broken. In South Africa we understood that true peace could be built only on the basis of justice and an unwavering commitment to universal rights for all humans, regardless of ethnicity, religion, gender, national origin or any other identity attribute. I encourage TIAA-CREF, whose slogan is 'for the greater good, to heed the call for divestment.'"[2]

Others have echoed this call. In the fall of 2012 a Jewish news agency revealed that the Swedish Arts Council had allocated nearly nine thousand dollars to help distribute a book promoting the apartheid agenda. First published earlier that year, it was written by Ingmar Karlsson. The retired Swedish diplomat says, "The fundamental difference between South African and Zionist colonialism is the former wanted land and people while the latter only wanted land."[3]

Another example is Richard Falk, a former professor of

international law at Princeton University and the United
Nations special rapporteur on the Palestinian territo-
ries. After addressing the UN Human Rights Council in
Geneva, Switzerland, in July of 2012, Falk told reporters
that Palestinian Authority Arabs in areas of Judea and
Samaria are offered no protection under Israeli law and
compared their treatment to apartheid: "'I think one has
to begin to call the reality by a name,' Falk said.... He lik-
ened the 'discriminatory dualistic legal system' in Judea
and Samaria to the former system in South Africa. In his
report to the council, Falk expressed his concern about
Israel's use of administrative detention, the expansion of
Jewish communities in the region and violence by local
Jewish residents."[4]

Simplifying the Complex

Before leaping to conclusions, those exploring this issue
must dig deeper than the daily headlines. For one, it is
worth noting that in 2011 the United States and American
Jewish groups called on the UN to discharge Falk after
he posted an anti-Semitic cartoon on his blog (hardly a
voice of impartiality). And as much as I respect Bishop
Tutu, I think he ignores some realities about life in Israel.
For one, all Israeli citizens—regardless of race, religion,
or gender—have equal protection under Israeli law. All
Israelis enjoy freedom of religion and speech and have
full voting rights. They work together, study together, and
visit one another's homes.

There are Arab-Israeli members of Israel's Parliament,
an Arab-Israeli member of Israel's Supreme Court, and

Arab-Israeli officers in Israel's uniformed services. As Reda Mansour, a former Israeli consul general and an Arab, says: "The freest Arabs in the Middle East reside in the Jewish state of Israel."[5]

Among others who have witnessed the situation up close and tell a much different story than the apartheid lobby is Richard Goldstone, a former justice of the South African Constitutional Court who led a UN fact-finding mission on the Gaza conflict of 2008–2009. In an op-ed published in the *New York Times* he called the apartheid claims against Israel a "particularly pernicious and enduring canard" and an "unfair and inaccurate slander against Israel, calculated to retard rather than advance peace negotiations."[6]

Noting that there are many facets to the Israeli-Arab conflict, Goldstone said it is important to distinguish between the situation in Israel (where Arabs are citizens) and West Bank areas that remain under Israeli control in the absence of a peace agreement between Israel and Palestinian leaders. Even with the latter, the situation is complex: what Palestinians see as oppression, Jews see as measures necessary for self-defense because of the ongoing threat of attacks from terrorists. The use of the offensive apartheid analogy and superficial attempts to distort reality are only damaging any prospects for peace, Goldstone wrote.

"Jewish-Arab relations in Israel and the West Bank cannot be simplified to a narrative of Jewish discrimination," he concluded. "There is hostility and suspicion on both sides. Israel, unique among democracies, has been in a state of war with many of its neighbors who refuse to accept its existence. Even some Israeli Arabs, because they are citizens of Israel, have at times come under suspicion from other Arabs as a result of that longstanding enmity. The mutual recognition and protection of the human dignity of all people is indispensable to bringing an end to hatred and anger. The charge that Israel is an apartheid state is a false and malicious one that precludes, rather than promotes, peace and harmony."[7]

Apartheid? When Israel airlifted tens of thousands of Ethiopian Jews to Israel in 1991, it made the history books. This courageous action marked the only time in human history that a nation transported thousands of Africans to its shores—not to condemn them to lifetimes of slavery, I might add, but to welcome them as free people and full citizens. This kind of action alone calls into question any comparisons between Israel and apartheid South Africa.

The use of the word *apartheid* in an Israeli context cheapens the evil of that system and discounts the suffering of those who lived under it. When it comes to Palestinians living in the West Bank and Gaza, Tutu argues that they are subject to all manner of oppression and injustice. Some of his claims, such as Palestinian "humiliation" at checkpoints, are mere exaggeration. Others, such as forced eviction and racial segregation, are patently untrue.

A History Primer

The foundation of Tutu's claim is that Israel is an aggressor occupying Palestinian land and the source of the ongoing conflict. Yet such a facile claim ignores history. The fact is that on five separate occasions—as recently as 2008—the Israelis have offered to split the land of Israel and Palestine with the Palestinians to have two states, one Jewish and one Arab. They would live side by side in peace. Each time the Arabs rejected the offer. It is the Arab rejection of a Jewish state anywhere in the Middle East that drives this conflict to the present day.

To recall the past, immediately upon the modern founding of Israel in 1948 (before Israel possessed either Gaza or the West Bank) Palestinians and Arabs in five neighboring states attacked Israel in an effort to destroy the nascent Jewish state. After that effort failed, in 1967 the Arabs tried again. The reason Israeli troops entered the West Bank and Gaza in the first place was to defend their nation from this attack. The Israelis decided not to return this land until they received a guarantee of peace in exchange. Yet Israel's withdrawal from most of the West Bank in the 1990s and all of Gaza in 2005 has not resulted in peace, but only more terrorist attacks. Israel continues to "occupy" the West Bank and Gaza because of adamant Palestinian refusal to stop the terror and sign an agreement that recognizes Israel's right to exist as a Jewish state.

Of course, we should not ignore the plight of the Palestinians. Many suffer in refugee camps in Lebanon, Syria, and Egypt and fail to enjoy equal rights with the citizens of those countries. Yet we cannot simplistically blame all of their suffering on Israel. Instead we must blame their grandparents and parents who rejected (and continue to reject) various offers for peace and independence that would end this decades-long conflict. In short, it is not Israel that oppresses Palestinians. It is the Palestinians leaders who continue to oppress their own people.

Furthermore, if Bishop Tutu and others throwing stones at Israel want to talk about a true apartheid state, they will have to explain the repressive actions of various Middle Eastern governments. They can start with dictators in Syria and Libya who have engaged in the ruthless killing of their own citizens. And less than a year after the overthrow of Muammar Gaddafi in October of 2011, the new Libyan government failed to protect the American ambassador and three other diplomatic personnel from deadly Islamist militants' attacks.

Then there is Iran, which can easily be characterized as an apartheid state. President Ahmadinejad continually oppresses any and all demonstrators that stand against the country's staunch Islamic regime. Only after continued, intense international diplomatic pressure did Iran release Pastor Yousef Nadarkhani from prison in September 2012 three years after he was incarcerated for the "crime" of apostasy. However, freeing Nadarkhani didn't signal the onset of freedom for Iranians. A month later security officials raided a prayer meeting and detained seven members of the same denomination, which sources close to Christian Solidarity Worldwide said were part of an upsurge in a campaign of harassment against all Christians.

"We particularly deplore the nature of the charges that are currently being leveled against Christians and other religious minorities," says Mervyn Thomas, Christian Solidarity Worldwide's CEO. "There appears to be an increasing tendency by the Iranian authorities to characterize legitimate religious activities as crimes against the state.... By arresting Christians who have peaceably gathered to pray or worship, Iran is violating their right to manifest their religious belief. We urge the Iranian government to end the harassment of religious minorities within its borders, to respect their right to freedom of religion, and to release all who have been held on account of their faith immediately and unconditionally."[8]

Saudi Arabia is another Middle Eastern nation lacking freedom of religion, freedom of speech, and freedom of assembly. In Saudi Arabia women are still considered second-class citizens under the law. In fact, Saudi Arabia is the only country in the world that prohibits women from legally driving. It is no surprise that women have few rights there, as demonstrated by a recent story about a thirty-year-old mother who served seven months in jail for disobeying her father.

Human Rights Watch exposed the case of Samar Badawi, who ended up in jail after she sought protection at a women's shelter. She had endured years of abuse by her father following her mother's death. In as outrageous an example of discrimination as I have ever read about, Badawi's father then brought a case against her for "disobedience." Saudi Arabia's guardianship laws gave him that opportunity, since they require women to gain permission from their father, husband, or even an adult son for many daily activities.

"I went in a broken woman," she said after her release. "I was very hurt when I went to prison. But I came out victorious and was very proud of myself that I was able to handle those seven months. It wasn't easy.... When I was alone, I would remember the injustice, from my father, from the judge who was horrible to me."[9]

I could go on at length, but I feel compelled to mention just one more example that is especially egregious. A teenage girl in Pakistan was recently shot in the head after promoting education for females and criticizing the Taliban. As she recovered at a hospital in London, Taliban leaders declared their desire to finish the job by not only killing her but also her father.[10] Yet it is Israel—a tiny strip of land the size of New Jersey—that the world wants to label and condemn as an apartheid state that oppresses its citizens and those living in the land? Such an idea is so preposterous that I must protest!

Israel is not perfect, but Africans from Egypt and Eritrea risk their lives every day seeking refuge and asylum in Israel's borders. They risk rape, attacks, and even murder...to live and work in an apartheid state? There are Arabs and Muslims who dream of obtaining Israeli citizenship—because Israel is the most free and democratic nation in the Middle East.

While Bishop Tutu and other critics of Israel eschew violence, their efforts are part of an international war of attrition on this sovereign nation's prosperity and legitimacy. Through boycott and divestment Tutu and his allies are attempting to harm Israel's blossoming economy. By calling into question Israel's right to defend itself against terrorism and negotiate defensible borders (by supporting

Palestinian unilateral action), they are denying Israel the very rights to which every other country is entitled.

The real problem in the Middle East is the Arab refusal to recognize and live in peace with Israel. By helping to delegitimize and marginalize Israel, those promoting the apartheid illusion do not foster peace. Instead they are giving hope and comfort to the rejectionist forces that have prolonged the conflict for more than six decades and show no signs of stopping. While the apartheid apologists may have good intentions, the impact is the exact opposite of what they profess to want—freedom and peace for the Palestinian people. Only when international critics shed their false claims against Israel can there be a solution to the problems Palestinians face. In the meantime, those who believe that God makes lasting covenants with His children must stand by the Jewish people.

CONCLUSION

THE AFRICAN AMERICAN church is a great reservoir of wisdom, wealth, and influence. It is my prayer and passionate pursuit that we will see the African American church use its power to fulfill its biblical responsibility to voice strong support of Israel. The Jewish community greatly needs the African American church, just as the African American community needed the support of the Jewish community during the 1950s and 1960s. As I outlined earlier, these two communities have parallel experiences of past pain. It is my prayer that this book has enlightened African American churches and communities about the importance of supporting Israel, regardless of a particular church's background, denomination, or tradition.

One of the most significant moments in my calling as an African American Christian Zionist came when I sat at the table of Prime Minister Benjamin Netanyahu. This phenomenal opportunity to meet privately with the prime minister opened for our group during a pastors' and ministry leaders' tour of Israel in 2008. I think of it as the "Table of Greatness." Not because of who the prime minister was or what he represented, even though this was extremely important. Not because of the wonderful leadership and presence of Pastor and Mrs. John Hagee; that too was priceless. For me, the most significant element of the evening originated with the presence of six African American pastors at this table.

During this briefing I heard several conversations concerning Christians' love and support for Israel. Though honored and humbled to be part of the group, I was more grateful to God for allowing me to help bring other African American leaders to the table of one of the most powerful, important men in the world. There discussions continued concerning the power of solidarity and unity between Christians and Jews.

I have long desired to see African Americans in the church recognized and respected for our gifts and contributions. For centuries African American churches were best known for the passion captured in our preaching and worship styles. We were known primarily for the energy we brought to the worship experience—our singing, shouting, and dancing; we were "happy, clappy Christians" who loved to wave tambourines.

Even during community and multicultural worship services I have watched as African American believers have graciously sung in the choir, ushered in the sanctuary, cooked in the kitchens, or provided security in the parking lots. I am proud to be part of a church that inspires such a servant's heart in its members, but I can't help but feel the body of Christ often misses out on all the other strengths we bring to the table. I believe we also deserve recognition for the strategic planning, critical thinking, and prayerful wisdom we bring to projects. We have become a strong, vital institution—despite slavery and decades of Jim

Crow discrimination—thanks to the efforts of incredible, capable leaders. The gifts we have within our churches were not meant to benefit our community alone.

The African American church must continue to be a place that is intellectually vigorous, morally courageous, and socially conscientious. We must care for the needs at home, and we must also look beyond the borders of our own economic and social well-being. We must remain steadfast and committed to defending the new social injustices of our time. Whether that is alleviating poverty, fighting HIV-AIDS, defending the pro-life cause, standing for traditional marriage and against human sex trafficking, or promoting justice in Darfur, Sudan, and Tibet, we must speak up and take action.

Then there are God's covenant people. The church must aggressively and courageously move forward here too, using its might and influence to support Israel and the Jewish community. I believe a table of greatness awaits African Americans willing to take such a stand. We can rebuild the bridges of commonality and cultural appreciation that existed prior to and during the civil rights era. The church's support will add strength and encouragement for Israel, and in blessing Israel we too will be blessed.

Today Christian support for Israel and the Jewish community is miraculously stretching beyond the borders of the United States and into international waters. The spring of 2012 marked Christians United for Israel's first "A Night to Honor Israel" held outside the United States. More than one thousand people from the east African nation of Kenya came together to celebrate Israel and the beloved Jewish community. The event was held in Nairobi the day after the Holocaust Memorial Day service was conducted at Kenya's only Jewish synagogue and community center.

Israel's ambassador to Africa, Gil Haskel, was a featured speaker at the event. Expressing his appreciation to the Kenyan people for their unwavering support for Israel, the Israeli ambassador commented, "Past blind hatred forced the Jews away from any relationship with the Christian community; however, blind love occurring in our lifetime is drawing them back in making a better future."[1]

Ironically, "A Night to Honor Israel" in Nairobi occurred in the midst of two separate terrorist bombing attacks against Christian churches in Kenya. Despite the security concerns of holding a pro-Israel event, the Kenyan Christian community courageously stood with Israel. Both Christians and Jews fully understood that they could not change the history of Jewish-Christian relations as it relates to Christian anti-Semitism, but they could mark the beginning of a new, positive chapter between our respective faith communities.

Today it becomes increasingly important for Christians both in Kenya and around the world to show the Jewish people and the State of Israel that they are not alone. We are called to act as modern-day Mordecais and Esthers who will urgently tell a generation of Christians the importance of lovingly standing with the Jews. The Hebrew word *tachless* embodies this determination and resolve. *Tachless* is a term that represents a no-nonsense, nonnegotiable, do-something-about-it attitude. It means roughly "all-or-nothing."

I've noticed that Israelis have a *tachless* mentality, which often manifests itself in their use of language—particularly the command. This *tachlessness* is surely bred from the kind of society in which they live. Constantly threatened, they realize the precariousness of life. This is what the Jews understood during the civil rights era: don't just talk about the problem; *do something*.

I recently presented a pro-Israel seminar titled "Understanding Better Why Christians Are Standing With Israel" at a South Florida Jewish synagogue. Near the end an older woman with a weak, frail voice, stood in the back of the room and shared these very moving words: "I am a Holocaust survivor from Auschwitz. When I was there, no one stood with us. Thank God for you for being here tonight. We're no longer alone as Jews. You're standing with us."

I intend to stand with her and millions of others just like her. I am *doing something*. Will you?

Notes

Preface

1. Daniel J. Goldhagen, *A Moral Reckoning* (New York: Alfred A. Knopf, 2002), 70.

2. David Brog, *Standing With Israel* (Lake Mary, FL: FrontLine, 2006), 37.

3. Elliott Abrams, *Faith or Fear* (New York: The Free Press, 1997), 46, as quoted in Brog, *Standing With Israel*, 37.

4. Brog, *Standing With Israel*, 37.

5. Abrams, *Faith or Fear*, 51.

6. Daniel C. Juster, "Why Israel Still Matters," *Charisma*, June 19, 2009, http://www.charismamag.com/blogs/standing -with-israel/5825-for-zions-sake-why-israel-still-matters (accessed January 4, 2013).

7. Paul E. Lovejoy, "The Impact of Atlantic Slave Trade on Africa: A Review of the Literature," *Journal of African History* 30, no. 3 (November 1989): 365–394.

Introduction

1. Jewish Virtual Library, "When the Rabbis Marched on Washington," http://www.jewishvirtuallibrary.org/jsource/ Holocaust/march.html (accessed January 4, 2013).

2. Library of Congress, "Today in History: March 7—First March From Selma," http://memory.loc.gov/ammem/today/ mar07.html (accessed January 4, 2013).

3. Susannah Heschel, "Following in My Father's Footsteps: Selma 40 Years Later," *Vox*, April 4, 2005, http://www .dartmouth.edu/~vox/0405/0404/heschel.html (accessed January 4, 2013).

4. Shai Held, Melissa Weintraub, and Yehuda Mirsky, "Heschel for a New Generation," *Tikkun* 22, no. 1 (January/ February 2007): 53–63.

5. Susannah Heschel, "Praying With Their Feet: Remembering Abraham Joseph Heschel and Martin Luther King," *Peacework*, December 2006–January 2007, http://www.peaceworkmagazine.org/praying-their-feet-remembering-abraham-joshua-heschel-and-martin-luther-king (accessed January 4, 2013).

6. *Moment Magazine*, "Jews and Blacks in America," January/February 2009, http://oldsite.momentmag.net/moment/issues/2009/02/Jews-Blacks-4.html (accessed February 15, 2013).

7. Steven Silbiger, *The Jewish Phenomenon: Seven Keys to the Enduring Wealth of a People* (Lanham, MD: Longstreet Press, 2002), 48.

8. Wikipedia.org, s.v. "National Association for the Advancement of Colored People," http://en.wikipedia.org/wiki/National_Association_for_the_Advancement_of_Colored_People (accessed January 4, 2013).

9. *Moment Magazine*, "Jews and Blacks in America," http://oldsite.momentmag.net/moment/issues/2009/02/Jews-Blacks-4.html (accessed January 4, 2013).

10. Ibid., http://oldsite.momentmag.net/moment/issues/2009/02/Jews-Blacks-1.html.

11. Harold Brackman, "Jews, African Americans, and Israel: The Ties That Bind," for Simon Wiesenthal Center/Museum of Tolerance, January/February 2010, http://www.wiesenthal.com/atf/cf/%7B54d385e6-f1b9-4e9f-8e94-890c3e6dd277%7D/THE_TIES_THAT_BIND_BRACKMAN.PDF (accessed January 4, 2013).

Chapter 1
Why Support Israel?

1. Trent C. Butler, ed., "Abraham," in *Holman Bible Dictionary* (Nashville: Holman Bible Publishers, 1991), 10.

2. E. A. Speiser, *Genesis*, in The Anchor Bible, vol. 1 (New York: Doubleday, 1964), 87.

3. Marvin R. Wilson, *Our Father Abraham: Jewish Roots of the Christian Faith* (Grand Rapids, MI: Eerdmans Publishing Company, 1989), 32.

4. James D. G. Dunn, *The Partings of the Ways: Between Christianity and Judaism and Their Significance for the Character of Christianity* (Philadelphia: Trinity Press International, 1991), 21.

5. Wilson, *Our Father Abraham*, 12.

6. W. Eugene March, *Great Themes of the Bible*, vol. 1 (Louisville, KY: Westminster John Knox Press, 2007), 12.

7. James Newell, "Covenant," in Butler, ed., *Holman Bible Dictionary*, 308.

8. Wilson, *Our Father Abraham*, 32.

9. Butler, ed., *Holman Bible Dictionary*, 309.

10. Kent Harold Richards, "Bless/Blessing," in David Noel Freedman, ed., *Anchor Bible Dictionary*, vol. 1 (New York: Doubleday, 1992), 755–756.

11. R. Laird Harris, Gleason Leonard Archer, and Bruce K. Waltke, *Theological Wordbook of the Old Testament*, electronic edition (Chicago: Moody Press, 1999), 132.

12. John N. Oswalt, "The Book of Isaiah, Chapters 40–66," in *New International Commentary on the Old Testament* (Grand Rapids, MI: Eerdmans, 1998), 584–585.

13. Carl F. Keil and Franz Delitzsch, "Isaiah," in *Commentary on the Old Testament.* (Peabody, MA: Hendrickson, 2002), 437.

14. Bill T. Arnold and Bryan E. Beyer, *Encountering the Old Testament: A Christian Survey* (Grand Rapids, MI: Baker Books, 1999), 378.

15. Douglas K. Stuart, *Old Testament Exegesis: A Handbook for Students and Pastors*, 4th ed. (Louisville, KY: Westminster John Knox Press, 2009), 28.

16. Arnold and Beyer, *Encountering the Old Testament*, 378.

17. Craig S. Keener, *The IVP Bible Background Commentary* (Downers Grove, IL: Intervarsity Press, 1993), 206.

18. Michael J. Wilkins, "Brother, Brotherhood," in Freedman, ed., *Anchor Bible Dictionary*, vol. 1, 782.

19. Keener, *The IVP Bible Background Commentary*, 118.

20. W. Eugene March, *Great Themes of the Bible*, vol. 1 (Louisville, KY: Westminster John Knox Press, 2007), 105.

21. Lance Lambert, *Israel: The Unique Land, the Unique People* (Wheaton, IL: Tyndale House Publishers, 1980), 58.

22. Joseph A. Fitzmyer, *The Gospel According to Luke, X–XXIV*, in The Anchor Bible (New York: Doubleday, 1985), 1008.

23. Lambert, *Israel: The Unique Land, the Unique People*, 59.

24. W. F. Albright and C. S. Mann, "Matthew," in *The Anchor Bible*, 119–120.

25. Fitzmyer, *The Gospel According to Luke, X–XXIV*, in The Anchor Bible, 256.

26. Ibid., 257.

27. Walid Shoebat, *Why I Left Jihad: The Root of Terrorism and the Rise of Islam* (New York: Top Executive Media, 2005), 191.

28. Robert Haldane, *An Exposition of Romans*, electronic edition (Simpsonville, SC: Christian Classics Foundation, 1996).

29. Dunn, *The Partings of the Ways*, 85.

30. N. T. Wright, *Jesus, Paul and the People of God: A Theological Dialogue With N. T. Wright*, Nicholas Perrin and Richard B. Hays, ed. (Downers Grove, IL: InterVarsity Press Academic, 2011), 265.

Chapter 2
Understanding Christian Zionism

1. D. A. Rausch, "Zionism," in Walter A. Elwell, ed., *Evangelical Dictionary of Theology* (Grand Rapids, MI: Baker Books, 1984), 1201.

2. Timothy P. Weber, *The Road to Armageddon: How Evangelicals Became Israel's Best Friend* (Grand Rapids, MI: Baker Books, 2004), 298.

3. John R. Stott, "The Place of Israel," as quoted in Stephen Sizer, "John R. Stott: The Place of Israel," July 31, 2011, http://www.stephensizer.com/2011/07/john-stott-the-place-of -israel/ (accessed January 7, 2013).

4. Brog, *Standing With Israel*, 80–81.

5. Ibid., 83.

6. Abrams, *Faith or Fear*, 68.

7. John Hagee speech at the Israeli embassy, December 14, 2002, as quoted in Brog, *Standing With Israel*, 73.

8. Jennifer Rubin, "Onward, Christian Zionists," *The Weekly Standard*, August 2, 2010, http://www.weeklystandard .com/print/articles/onward-Christian-Zionists (accessed January 7, 2013).

9. Ibid.

10. Wilson, *Our Father Abraham*, 12–13.

11. Ibid., 30.

12. Ibid.

13. Paul P. Enns, *The Moody Handbook of Theology* (Chicago: Moody Press, 1997), 615.

14. Ibid., 616.

15. Abrams, *Faith or Fear*, 53.

16. Ronald Diprose, *Israel and the Church: The Origin and Effects of Replacement Theology* (Milton Keynes, UK: Authentic Media, 2004), 169.

17. *Dialogue With Trypho*, cited in Brog, *Standing With Israel*, 21.

18. As cited in Rosemary Ruether, *Faith and Fratricide* (Eugene: Wipf and Stock Publishers, 1995), 146–147.

19. Augustine, *City of God* (London: Penguin, 1972), 828, as cited in Brog, *Standing With Israel*, 23.

20. Lambert, *Israel: The Unique Land, the Unique People*, 53–54.

21. John Hagee, *Should Christians Support Israel?* (San Antonio, TX: Dominion Publishers, 1987), 23.

22. Norman P. Tanner, ed. and trans., "Constitution 68: Jews Appearing in Public," *Decrees of the Ecumenical Councils*, Fourth Lateran Council (1215), Eternal Word Television Network, http://www.ewtn.com/library/COUNCILS/LATERAN4.HTM (accessed January 7, 2013).

23. As quoted in Hagee, *Should Christians Support Israel?*, 18–19.

24. Diprose, *Israel and the Church*, 171.

25. Hagee, *Should Christians Support Israel?*, 5.

Chapter 3
Educating Others

1. Walter A. Elwell, "Dietrich Bonhoeffer," in R. Zerner, ed., *Evangelical Dictionary of Theology* (Grand Rapids, MI: Baker Books, 1984), 168.

2. As quoted in *Bonhoeffer: Pastor, Pacifist, Nazi Resister*, documentary by Martin Doblmeier (New York: First Run Features, 2003), DVD.

3. Josiah U. Young, *Bonhoeffer's Intellectual Formation*, Peter Frick, ed. (Tubingen: Mohr Siebeck, 2008), 292.

4. *Bonhoeffer: Pastor, Pacifist, Nazi Resister*.

5. Ibid.

6. Ibid.

7. Eberhard Bethge, Renate Bethge, and Christia Gremmels, eds., *Dietrich Bonhoeffer: A Life in Pictures* (Berlin: SCM Press, 1986), 98.

8. Ronald H. Stone, *Professor Reinhold Niebuhr: A Mentor to the Twentieth Century* (Louisville, KY: Westminster/John Knox Press, 1992), xii.

9. Ibid., 262.

10. Ibid.

11. Karl Barth, "Starting Out, Turning Round, Confessing," in *Final Testimonies*, Eberhard Busch, ed., Geoffrey W. Bomiley,

trans. (Grand Rapids, MI: Eerdmans, 1977), as quoted by
Joseph L. Mangina, *Karl Barth: Theologian of Christian Witness*
(London: Westminster John Knox Press, 2004), 4.

12. Rolf Joachim Erler and Reiner Marquard, *A Karl Barth
Reader* (Grand Rapids, MI: Eerdmans Publishing Company,
1986), 70–71.

13. Ibid.

14. Ibid., 14.

15. Ibid.

16. Wilson, *Our Father Abraham*, 270–271.

17. Ibid., 273.

18. Ibid.

19. Ibid.

Chapter 4
The Role of the African American Church

1. Pew Forum on Religion and Public Life, "A Religious
Portrait of African-Americans," January 30, 2009, http://www
.pewforum.org/A-Religious-Portrait-of-African
-Americans.aspx (accessed January 8, 2013).

2. Ibid.

3. Ibid.

4. Ibid.

5. Ibid.

6. C. Eric Lincoln and Lawrence H. Mamiya, *The Black
Church in the African American Experience* (Durham, NC:
Duke University Press, 1990), 18.

7. Ibid., 17.

8. Ibid.

9. Ibid.

10. James H. Cone, "Black Theology and the Black Church:
Where Do We Go From Here?" quoted in Milton C. Sernett,
ed., *Afro-American Religious History* (Durham, NC: Duke
University Press, 1985), 477.

11. Peter Paris, "The Black Christian Tradition," quoted in Peter C. Hodgson and Robert H. King, eds., *Readings in Christian Theology* (Philadelphia: Fortress Press, 1985), 255.

12. James P. Eckman, *Exploring Church History* (Wheaton, IL: Crossway, 2002), 98.

13. Ibid., 99.

14. Paris, "The Black Christian Tradition," in *Readings in Christian Theology*, 255.

15. Lincoln and Mamiya, *The Black Church in the African American Experience*, 97.

16. Martin Luther King Jr., "Social Justice and the Emerging New Age," speech given at Herman W. Read Fieldhouse, Western Michigan University, December 18, 1963, as quoted in *Famous Quotes From 100 Great People* (n.p.: MobileReference, 2011). Viewed at Google Books.

17. Jonathan Rieder, *The Word of the Lord Is Upon Me: The Righteous Performance of Martin Luther King, Jr.* (Cambridge, MA: Harvard University Press, 2008), 290.

18. I. L. Kenen, *Israel's Defense Line*, (Buffalo, NY: Prometheus Books, 1981), 266.

19. Rieder, *The Word of the Lord Is Upon Me*, 290.

20. Ibid., 291.

Chapter 5
Void of a Voice: Misleading the African American Community

1. Jason Horowitz, "Obama Addresses Homophobia, Anti-Semitism and Xenophobia Among Black Americans," *New York Observer*, January 20, 2008, http://observer.com/2008/01/obama-addresses-homophobia-antisemitism-and-xenophobia-among-black-americans/ (accessed January 8, 2013).

2. Sol Roth, "Black Anti-Semitism: Diagnosis and Treatment," *Judaism* 30, no. 3 (Summer 1981): 285.

3. Abrams, *Faith or Fear*, 159.

4. Brackman, "Jews, African Americans, and Israel: The Ties That Bind."

5. Joshua Muravchik, "Facing Up to Black Anti-Semitism," *Commentary* magazine, December 1, 1995.

6. Ibid.

7. Christopher Reardon, "African-Americans and Jews Rebuild a Tattered Alliance," *Christian Science Monitor*, April 17, 1996, http://www.csmonitor.com/1996/0417/17014.html (accessed January 8, 2013).

8. PBS.org, "From Swastika to Jim Crow: Black-Jewish Relations," http://www.pbs.org/itvs/fromswastikatojimcrow/relations.html (accessed January 8, 2013).

9. Roth, "Black Anti-Semitism: Diagnosis and Treatment," 285.

10. Ibid., 286.

11. Ibid., 288.

12. Muravchik, "Facing Up to Black Anti-Semitism."

13. Eric J. Sundquist, *Strangers in the Land: Blacks, Jews, Post-Holocaust America* (Cambridge, MA: Harvard University Press, 2005), 8.

14. Larry J. Sabato, "Jesse Jackson's 'Hymietown' Remark—1984, *Washington Post*, http://www.washingtonpost.com/wp-srv/politics/special/clinton/frenzy/jackson.htm (accessed January 8, 2013).

15. Kenneth R. Timmerman, *Shakedown: Exposing the Real Jesse Jackson* (Washington DC: Regnery Publishing, 2002), 148.

16. Ibid., 161.

17. Edward Shapiro, *Crown Heights: Blacks, Jews, and the 1991 Brooklyn Riot* (Lebanon, NH: Brandeis University Press, 2006).

18. JewishJournal.com, "Yankel Rosenbaum's Brother: Sharpton Shouldn't Be on Shul's Crown Heights Panel," August 18, 2011, http://www.jewishjournal.com/nation/

article/yankel_rosenbaums_brother_sharpton_shouldnt_be_
on_shuls_crown_hts_panel_20/ (accessed January 8, 2013).

19. Ibid.

20. JewishJournal.com, "Al Sharpton: I Made 'Mistakes'
During Crown Heights Riots," August 22, 2011, http://www
.jewishjournal.com/nation/article/al_sharpton_i_made
_mistakes_during_crown_heights_riots_20110822 (accessed
January 8, 2013).

21. David Squires, "Rev. Jeremiah Wright Says 'Jews' Are
Keeping Him From President Obama," *Daily Press* (Hampton
Roads, VA), June 10, 2009, http://www.dailypress.com/news/
dp-local_wright_0610jun10,0,7603283.story (accessed January
8, 2013), quoted in Dexter Van Zile, "Mainline American
Christian 'Peacemakers' Against Israel," Jerusalem Center
for Public Affairs, November 5, 2009, http://jcpa.org/article/
mainline-american-christian-peacemakers-against-israel/
(accessed January 8, 2013).

22. Michael C. Kotzin, "Louis Farrakhan's Anti-Semitism:
A Look at the Record," *The Christianity Century*, vol. 111, no. 7,
March 2, 1994, 226.

23. Abrams, *Faith or Fear*, 159.

24. Kotzin, "Louis Farrakhan's Anti-Semitism: A Look at
the Record," 224.

25. Muravchik, "Facing Up to Black Anti-Semitism."

26. Brackman, "Jews, African Americans, and Israel: The
Ties That Bind."

27. Ibid.

28. Timmerman, *Shakedown: Exposing the Real Jesse
Jackson*, 109.

29. Author interview with Lemuel Thuston, bishop and
church historian in the Church of God in Christ, Orlando,
Florida, August 25, 2011.

30. James L. Guth, "Religious Leadership and Support for
Israel: A Study of Clergy in Nineteen Denominations," presented at the annual meeting of the Southern Political Science

Association, Hotel Intercontinental, New Orleans, Louisiana, January 3–7, 2007, http://www.furman.edu/depts/ps/faculty/guth/Publications/New%20Orleans%20Paper.pdf (accessed January 8, 2013).

31. Alan Dershowitz, *The Case for Israel* (Hoboken, NJ: John Wiley and Sons, 2003), 221.

32. "The Right of Return: An Interview With Benny Morris," *Tikkun* 16, no. 2 (March/April 2001): 18.

33. Dore Gold, "Countdown to September: Israel, the Palestinians, and the UN General Assembly," Jerusalem Center for Public Affairs, May 1, 2011, http://jcpa.org/article/countdown-to-september-israel-the-palestinians-and-the-un-general-assembly/ (accessed January 8, 2013).

Chapter 6
Israel's Enemies Through the Ages

1. Arash Norouzi, "'Wiped Off the Map'—The Rumor of the Century," The Mossadegh Project, January 18, 2007, http://www.mohammadmossadegh.com/news/rumor-of-the-century/ (accessed January 8, 2013).

2. Glenn Kessler, "Did Ahmadinejad Really Say Israel Should Be 'Wiped Off the Map'?", *The Fact Checker* (blog), *Washington Post*, October 5, 2011, http://www.washingtonpost.com/blogs/fact-checker/post/did-ahmadinejad-really-say-israel-should-be-wiped-off-the-map/2011/10/04/gIQABJIKML_blog.html (accessed January 8, 2013).

3. JerusalemJournal.com, "Morsi Answers Amen to Imam's Prayers for Destruction of Jews," October 22, 2012, http://www.jewishjournal.com/world/article/morsi_answers_amen_to_imams_prayers_for_destruction_of_jews (accessed January 8, 2013).

4. Warren Cole Smith, "Stealth Jihadists," *World*, October 6, 2012; posted online September 21, 2012, http://www.worldmag.com/2012/09/stealth_jihadists (accessed January 8, 2013). Used with permission.

5. Ibid.

6. *Iranium*, directed by Alex Traiman (n.p.: Clarion Fund, 2011), documentary.

7. Ibid.

8. Kessler, "Did Ahmadinejad Really Say Israel Should Be 'Wiped Off the Map'?"

9. Nazila Fathi, "Wipe Israel 'Off the Map' Iranian Says," *New York Times*, October 27, 2005, http://www.nytimes.com/2005/10/26/world/africa/26iht-iran.html (accessed January 8, 2013).

10. Anti-Defamation League, "Terrorism: Muslim Brotherhood," http://www.adl.org/terrorism/symbols/muslim_brotherhood_1.asp (accessed January 8, 2013).

11. Art Moore, "'Son of Hamas' Warns U.S. Fatally Falling for Lies," *World Net Daily*, August 25, 2010, http://www.wnd.com/2010/08/194989/ (accessed January 8, 2013).

12. QuotationsBook.com, http://quotationsbook.com/quote/164/ (accessed October 9, 2012).

13. Kenen, *Israel's Defense Line*, 266.

Chapter 7
The Israel Apartheid Question

1. BBC News, "Tutu Condemns Israeli 'Apartheid,'" April 29, 2002, http://news.bbc.co.uk/2/hi/1957644.stm (accessed January 8, 2013).

2. Desmond Tutu, "For the Record: TIAA-CREF Should Hear Us, Divest From Israeli Apartheid," *Charlotte Observer*, July 17, 2011, 20A, as accessed at WeDivest.org, "Archbishop Desmond Tutu Endorses Campaign, Asks TIAA-CREF to Divest," http://wedivest.org/2011/07/archbishop-desmond-tutu-endorses-campaign-asks-tiaa-cref-to-divest/ (accessed January 8, 2013).

3. JTA.org, "Swedish Government Body Funding Book on Israeli 'Apartheid,'" October 12, 2012, http://www.jta.org/news/article/2012/10/12/3109101/swedish-government-body-funding-book-on-israeli-apartheid (accessed January 8, 2013).

4. Elad Benari, "UN 'Human Rights' Official Attacks Israeli 'Apartheid' Policy," IsraelNationalNews.com, July 3, 2012, http://www.israelnationalnews.com/News/News.aspx/157445#.UHwsHGeeiSp (accessed January 8, 2013).

5. Reda Mansour, "Israel Sets an Example of Freedom, Tolerance," *Atlanta Journal-Constitution*, February 5, 2007, accessed at From the Desk of Reda Mansour, http://redamansour.wordpress.com/2008/07/18/israel-sets-an-example-of-freedom-tolerance/ (accessed January 8, 2013).

6. Richard J. Goldstone, "Israel and the Apartheid Slander," *New York Times*, October 31, 2011, http://www.nytimes.com/2011/11/01/opinion/israel-and-the-apartheid-slander.html (accessed January 8, 2013).

7. Ibid.

8. Kiri Kankhwende, "Seven Christians Arrested During Prayer Meeting in Iran," Charisma News, October 16, 2012, http://www.charismanews.com/world/34325-seven-christians-arrested-during-prayer-meeting-in-iran (accessed January 8, 2013).

9. Rima Maktabi and Schams Elwazer, "Saudi Women: Pampered or Oppressed?", CNN.com, March 14, 2012, http://www.cnn.com/2012/03/14/world/meast/saudi-women-disagree-rights/index.html (accessed January 8, 2013).

10. BBC News, "Malala Yousafzai Leaves Queen Elizabeth Hospital," January 4, 2013, http://www.bbc.co.uk/news/uk-england-birmingham-20908439 (accessed January 8, 2013).

Conclusion

1. Remarks by Gil Haskel, A Night to Honor Israel event, Nairobi, Kenya, April 19, 2012, at which the author was present.

INDEX

About the Author

Dr. Michael A. Stevens Sr. is a man of God who passionately pursues the promises of the Father in heaven concerning life, success, and faithfulness. In 1994 he founded the University City Church of God in Christ. Beginning with only two members, this life-changing and impactful ministry has surpassed seventeen hundred members in just eighteen years of ministry in Charlotte, North Carolina.

Pastor Stevens has earned doctor of ministry and masters of practical theology degrees from Oral Roberts University and is a graduate of North Carolina A&T State University, where he received a bachelor's of science degree in political studies. Pastor Stevens serves on the executive boards of both the General Council of Pastors and Elders and the National Church Growth Conference of the Church of God in Christ. He is also the African American Outreach Director for Christians United for Israel (CUFI), the largest pro-Israel organization in the United States.

Pastor Stevens is committed to helping young leaders discover, develop, and walk in their purpose. He has been privileged to preach coast-to-coast and abroad in such countries as Bermuda, Kenya, Belize, Israel, Peru, and South Africa. He is the author of *Straight Up*, *No More Excuses*, and *Restoring the Order of Spiritual Fathers and Sons*.

Pastor Stevens resides in Charlotte, North Carolina, and is married to his college sweetheart, Sharon, and they have been blessed with three children. For more information, visit www.MichaelAStevens.com or www.UniversityCityChurch.tv.

CREDIBLE, RELEVANT COVERAGE
of the issues that **matter most to you**

FrontLine brings you books, e-books, and other media covering current world affairs and social issues from a Christian perspective. View all of FrontLine's releases at the links below and discover how to bring your values, faith, and biblical principles into today's marketplace of ideas.

FRONT LINE